THE COLD CASE
MURDER OF
FRED WILKERSON

Untangling the Black Widow's Web in West Georgia

CLAY BRYANT

Foreword by Tracie Wilkerson Campbell

THE
History
PRESS

Published by The History Press
Charleston, SC
www.historypress.com

First published 2023

Manufactured in the United States

ISBN 9781467154048

Library of Congress Control Number: 2022950086

CONTENTS

FOREWORD

y name is Tracie Wilkerson Campbell. I'm the daughter of a wonderful man, Fred Wilkerson, who was taken from us by an evil woman named Connie Quedens in 1987.

My family was the typical working-class family. My mother was a secretary at a local company for many years, and my daddy worked at a local distribution company most of my childhood. I am four years older than my brother, Tim Wilkerson. I am very proud that my parents instilled the love of family, commitment and integrity in Tim and me. My father was married to Carolyn, our mother, for twenty-two years. I was fortunate to enjoy a safe, secure and loving home life. Things were not always perfect, but they were pretty close to it in my eyes.

Life went on as Tim and I grew up and activities kept us busy. Daddy would drive me and my friends to these activities, and he would support my brother in baseball, Boy Scouts, whatever he was participating in at the time. He was a very involved parent and was a family man. One night in particular (before cellphones), I was working at Kroger and was eighteen or nineteen years old. I had worked a little late, and on my way home, I met him coming into town to look for me. That always was something I remembered; he was not someone who was "checking up on me," he was genuinely concerned about me.

When Connie was hired at the local distribution company Daddy worked at, things changed dramatically from that point. She was a very manipulative woman. Every time she had a crisis, she called Daddy to come resolve it. He worked the night shift for a week or so, and she called him several times during the day on our house phone. We would also experience hang-ups as we answered. Things changed in my parents' marriage also, and they separated. They tried to reconnect later, but it wasn't successful.

Tim was fifteen years old and I was nineteen years old when they divorced. It was hard. Mama took a second job and was left with two kids, a house and bills. I was attending LaGrange College and working, so I wasn't at home until late most evenings. It was a sad time for us. I was a little older to handle the change at home, but it was harder on Tim, as he and Daddy were very close. Suddenly, this woman seemed to be consuming our daddy. She had her own family, and I didn't understand.

Roger, my husband, helped me deal with all the mess. He, ironically, was working at NOK with Gary Quedens, Connie's husband, in 1987, when the disappearance occurred. I can't imagine how stressful this time had to be for him, but he was a trooper and handled the working relationship with Gary very professionally. He was my rock and helped me keep going. Sadly, he is now my guardian angel.

Connie was not like anyone I had met before. She seemed very competitive and outspoken. As sad as we were, this is who our daddy had chosen to be with, and quite frankly, she scared me. She talked to her children fiercely. One time, I stopped by the house they were building on Ware's Cross Road and her boys were there. Daddy was laying sod by the pool. I witnessed her cursing at her two boys, and I will never forget Daddy looking at me for several moments. I was thinking—as I felt he was, too—that neither he nor Mama spoke to Tim and me like that. But no words were necessary. I felt so bad for him that he was involved in all that. I still remember vividly the feeling of utter sickness I had that day.

I remember when I learned my daddy was missing. It was pure shock and disbelief—"Hold on, this can't be true." He would not go away without telling us or his mother where he was going. This was not typical of his character. He would drive to Roanoke, Alabama, to visit my grandmother every week, no matter how short the visit.

After his disappearance, we gathered at the apartment that Tim and Daddy shared. We set up search parties. We called everyone we knew. Flyers were printed for us to distribute with the sheriff's number on them. We set up an answering machine so that, hopefully, someone would call in with information. People helped search my grandmothers' property and surrounding areas to see if they could find him. Daddy, at this time, was driving for Fast Food Merchandisers, so a group retraced his route, which went as far as Andalusia, Alabama. We gave flyers to other truck drivers to distribute. One particular day, the sheriff's department even had me call Connie, who was at work at the Honda dealership. I asked her if she had seen my father or heard from him, and of course, she said no.

An empty feeling is created when someone just disappears into thin air. It's a feeling I would not wish on anyone. Sadly, we knew in our hearts that Connie was responsible for his disappearance. It is a time I hate to even recount. I was afraid to walk my dog outside in the dark. Fear of the unknown is tough.

We met with the investigators and sheriff's deputies during this time. There were no clues, only suspicion on our family's behalf. We also met with a GBI agent, hoping to elevate the investigation. There we were, two kids, desperate to find out what had happened to our daddy. I was twenty-three and Tim was nineteen at the time. All I remember at the time was the detective saying to us was that "he had seen cases like this before, Fred was under a lot of pressure and just walked away." We were adamant that Daddy would never walk away and leave his family. That was our chance to get the investigation elevated, but we left the meeting defeated.

Everywhere we went, the door was closed in our face. Each time, there were no clues—nothing. We were just two kids with a family and

Tracie Wilkerson Campbell at the search for her father's remains. *Author's collection.*

community who wanted the truth. When Daddy's car was found a month after his disappearance, we felt that, finally, this would give us some answers. But there were no fingerprints—nothing. With no clues evident, the case grew cold.

So, we had to go on with life, and that was not easy. During this time, we had to deal with never giving up hope on finding our father. That was tough to do. You never felt like you did enough—the dreams, the false reports of sightings. I credit my brother, who had much more tenacity than I did to keep Daddy's case in the forefront.

I believe in God's timing, and seventeen years later, when the case was reopened, it seemed that everything fell into place. I am thankful for the chain of events that led up to the arrest and conviction of Connie Quedens, the evil woman who took so much from us.

Since the case has been solved, several people of authority have said things to us as if they needed to clear their conscience because they either didn't or couldn't help us. I'm glad they could feel better as I carefully listened to them express their feelings of aggravation and disappointment. When I think back on that dark time, I am still frustrated and saddened. But it was just not meant to be then.

I feel cheated that Daddy never got to see Tim and me grow up and start families of our own. This evil woman is finally serving time for the crime she committed. She has come up for parole a couple of times, and fortunately, it has been denied each time.

Thank you, Clay, for forging ahead and not letting Connie threaten you. You surprised her this time, and your tireless work is appreciated. Thank you, Pete Skandalakis (district attorney at the time), for opening up the cold case. I'm sorry your truck was damaged by the fallen tree, but God works in mysterious ways and that was the start of everything. Thanks to all the other folks who worked on this case. For those who touched the investigation earlier on, thank you.

I remember when Clay started working with us. We piled all our documents, notes and data on the floor of Tim and his wife Laurie's house. Along with Clay, Tim, Laurie and Roger, I worked for many weeks, days and hours, poring over the timeline, documents, et cetera. Whatever we could provide for the investigation, we gave it. We spent time away from our children to bring justice to Daddy.

The trial lasted a week, and when the jury returned the guilty verdict, it was bittersweet. There's something to say about getting closure. As sad as it was to experience the outcome, it has been better knowing the truth. No one has the right to take someone else's life, and the only earthly thing we can do is hope they are punished in prison for the rest of their life. Justice was done.

To anyone reading this story who may now be waiting—as we were for seventeen years—never give up hope. When it is time, God will put it all into place, including the people to carry it out, and He will give you the strength to get through it. I am so thankful to Him.

Tracie Wilkerson Campbell
Philippians 4:13

INTRODUCTION

The black widow spider is common to the southeastern United States. Its name alone strikes fear in anyone who has knowledge of this venomous creature. The bite of the black widow is, at the least, extremely painful, and the neurotoxin in its venom can be fatal.

The black widow is very reclusive, spinning its web in dark, forbidding places as it lies in wait for its prey. The life of the female black widow is steeped in lore, legend and fact, based on her sinister mating ritual. She spins an intricate web hidden away from the eyes of the world; it is from this web that she entices her mate blindly into her realm. It is there they mate, and as soon as the male has made his contribution, the more dominant female turns on her mate, killing him, and proceeds to devour him.

Connie King Quedens spun webs of lies and deceit, fueled by her materialistic greed. Connie had no qualms whatsoever in using any means she felt necessary to achieve her desires.

Fred Wilkerson's personality made him the perfect victim for Connie's evil scheme. Fred was a trusting soul who would do just about anything to avoid conflict. Little did Fred know that his giving and trusting ways would cost him everything: his job, his family, everything he owned and, in the end, even his life—all because he was drawn into and entangled in the black widow's web.

1

FRIDAY NEVER CAME

The last time Tim and Tracie Wilkerson saw their father, Fred, was at Thanksgiving dinner in 1987 at the home of Fred's sister Jewell and her husband, Clarence Lee, on Sanders Road in LaGrange, Georgia. As the afternoon wore on, Fred, who drove a truck for Fast Food Merchandisers, told the family he was going home to get some sleep. He was to leave at five o'clock the next morning to make deliveries in Tennessee. This trip was somewhat special to Fred, as Tim was going to make the trip with him to keep him company, as he did occasionally when their schedules would allow it.

Tim and Tracie told their father goodbye, with Tim telling his dad he would be home later in the evening, as he was going to visit with some friends before they embarked on their trip the next morning. Little did they know that afternoon would be the last time they would see their father alive, beginning a seventeen-year-long journey of disappointment, frustration and heartbreak as they searched for their father and answers about what happened to him.

Tim got home to his and his father's apartment shortly after midnight on Friday, November 28, 1987, the day after Thanksgiving. He fully expected to find his father, Fred, asleep in the apartment upon his arrival, but to his surprise, Fred was not at home. At first, Tim wasn't overly concerned, as his dad was often gone for some reason or other when Tim got home, but he would always show up.

Fred Wilkerson. *Courtesy of Tim Wilkerson.*

Fred was never late or absent from work, and Tim was certain he'd be home in time for them to make their anticipated trip to Tennessee. Upon his arrival at home, Tim saw that Fred's clothes and trip bag were laid out for the morning. Fred had already told Tim they would leave the Fast Food Merchandisers warehouse at five o'clock in the morning to make their first unloading appointment. The schedule they had to keep was critical.

As the early morning hours wore on, Tim became more and more concerned. Three o'clock came and passed, then four o'clock, still with no sign of Fred. Tim could not envision his dad leaving without him, and he could not understand what could have happened. He began to have an ominous feeling that maybe something bad had happened to his father.

Tim hoped that his dad had just gotten caught up in whatever he was doing and realized he was going to be late and had just gone directly to the Fast Food warehouse. As five o'clock came and passed, Tim had an even stronger feeling that something was terribly wrong. Tim was now very worried and decided to go to the warehouse in hopes of finding his father there, getting ready to start their day. Upon arrival, Tim found Fred's loaded truck sitting behind the gate, awaiting its driver who would never come.

By now, Tim was frantic. He called his sister, Tracie, to find out if maybe she had heard from their father, but as Tim feared, she had not. After a few more agonizing hours passed, Tim went to the Troup County Sheriff's Office to report his father missing. There, he was told he could not file a missing person's report on an adult until at least forty-eight hours had elapsed since they were last seen. He returned home and began contacting friends and family members to see if anyone had heard anything from Fred. By now, every one of Fred's family members and his close friends were aware of his absence; most of them, knowing the situation Fred had been in, feared that perhaps he had run into an act of foul play or, because of the pressures he had been under, could have possibly taken his own life.

For the next two days, Fred's family and friends searched in vain for any sign or word of their loved one, but it was not to come. Sunday found Tim back at the sheriff's office, this time to successfully file a missing person's report on his father. Over the next several days, with no sign of Fred, the family began to organize searches and distributed flyers all over west-central Georgia and east Alabama to find any word on Fred. This futile search would continue for the next seventeen long years.

Fred had gotten involved with a woman at his previous workplace. That relationship resulted in Fred getting divorced from Carolyn, his wife of twenty-one years, and investing everything he had financially into twenty-

MISSING:
Fred Wilkerson

Age: 49
5 Ft. 9 In. Tall
160 Pounds
Black Hair / Blue Eyes

May be driving a champagne colored
1987 Honda Accord
Tag Number: PAG 205

Last seen in LaGrange, Georgia
Novemeber 27, 1987
CALL:
(404) 882-5159
or TROUP COUNTY SHERIFF'S
DEPARTMENT
(404) 883-1616

A missing person poster that was circulated during the frantic days after the disappearance of Fred Wilkerson. *Courtesy of Tim Wilkerson.*

three acres of land and what he thought would be a marital home for the woman he was involved with and himself. Instead, the relationship led to him losing everything. Fred's family and friends were distraught, as they were now certain that he had fallen victim to the black widow's web.

2

THE LONG ROAD TO NOWHERE

Hours turned into days, days into weeks, weeks into months and months into years, all with no credible word on the whereabouts of Fred Wilkerson. There were the occasional sightings of Fred, either by mistaken but well-intentioned friends and acquaintances or intentionally misleading individuals who, for whatever reason, just wanted to interject themselves into something they knew nothing about.

Throughout my career, I have occasionally run across those people who had an uncontrollable desire to involve themselves in serious investigations and either did not know or did not care how much damage their misinformation could do to the progress of the investigation. Sometimes, people, just like investigators, theorize what they believe the situation to be and convince themselves they know what has happened, and every time they explain their theory, it becomes more concrete in their minds and becomes fact to them.

I attribute much of my success as an investigator to the commonsense teachings of my dad, Buddy Bryant, who, in my eyes, was the best investigator I've ever known. I remember his words as we were discussing a case he was working. I stated what I thought, in my opinion, was an obvious conclusion. Daddy chuckled and said, "Son, I know you are highly intelligent and are sure you got this thing figured out and have a theory of exactly what and how this happened. The problem is, you are now in danger of seeking evidence to support your theory instead of objectively seeking evidence to carry you to the truth. Never find yourself falling into that trap." Some of the cold cases I have worked on came to me as the result of investigators falling victim to this snare and refusing to look beyond their own theories. This willful blindness not only hampered finding the factual resolution, but in some cases, it resulted in false suspicion that damaged the lives of innocent people. I can't truthfully say there haven't been times when I've been guilty of nearly becoming entangled in that trap myself, saved only by remembering my dad's words.

But in this case, it became clear to me that the initial investigation into the disappearance and murder of Fred Wilkerson fell headlong into that age-old trap.

I was lucky enough to have a very special relationship with my dad. He was my best friend, confidant and mentor. I truly believe some of best education I ever received came from the philosophy lessons of my dad. There was nothing we didn't talk about. I recollect one instance in particular when we were discussing romantic relationships, especially toxic ones, as we were riding along in my patrol car. Daddy looked over at me and said, "Son, love is but a dewdrop from heaven. The problem is that it had just as soon fall on a horse turd as a geranium." In the Fred Wilkerson case, Connie King Quedens sure as hell proved to be no geranium.

In my lifetime of investigation, I can guarantee that if you were to ask fifty random people about a fictitious event, such as a make-believe train robbery that occurred in town, you would probably have forty-nine sensible people who would truthfully say they had no knowledge of the event; however, there would be at least one fool who would look you straight in the eye and say, "Man, I was there and saw the whole damn thing." Now, you must expend precious time and resources to discredit this fairytale that is nothing more than the babblings of the village idiot, and all the while, the truth is slipping further and further away.

There were reported sightings of Fred on numerous occasions. There were reports from many places—some said he was just across the Alabama border, and another reported him getting off an elevator in Las Vegas. This report from Las Vegas even led officials to obtain video footage from the hotel where the sighting was reported by a gentleman who had been very familiar with Fred. The old adage that everyone has a body double turned out to be true in this case, as the video revealed yet another case of mistaken identity. These sightings, as well intended as most were, only contributed to the investigation of Fred's disappearance losing focus and prolonging the agony of those who were seeking answers to the question of what had happened to him.

To say that the investigation was stalled would be a fair assessment; however, investigators still monitored Fred's social security account for activity, but there was none. Early on, investigators followed every lead, sighting and bit of information that might have brought the truth to light—but to no avail.

The case of the disappearance and murder of Fred Wilkerson contained misinformation, disinformation and strong opinions and incorrect theories about Fred's disappearance, all contributing to what seemed like an endless nightmare for the Wilkerson family and the seventeen-year-long and winding road that would finally lead to the untangling of the black widow's web.

3

FROM HUMBLE BEGINNINGS

Alma and Zelmer Wilkerson were married and raised their family in one of the hardest times this country has ever seen: the Great Depression. Life was a struggle as they eked out a living on their family farm in Randolph County, Alabama, a mere stone's throw from the Heard County, Georgia line. The ground of red dirt was poor and rocky in the hills of eastern Randolph County, and pulling a living out of it was hard, if not nearly impossible. Zelmer found work as a carpenter and in construction anytime and anywhere to supplement the family's meager living. This would often leave Alma alone with the responsibilities of the farm. These problems weren't unique to the Wilkersons; everyone had to do what was necessary to survive.

Alma gave birth to their first child, a baby girl named Jewell, on August 23, 1929. Nine years would pass before the arrival of the next addition to the family, and on April 13, 1938, Willie Fred Wilkerson was born. Life was still challenging for the family in the post-Depression era, as Zelmer had to find work where he could, which was usually out of town, leaving the farm to be tended by Alma. No one was spared from the never-ending toil of raising a family. Jewell, at the age of nine, had to assume the role of mothering her baby brother while their mother worked in the field. It was a role she played for the rest of their lives. Perhaps because of these circumstances, there was a tremendous bond between Fred and Jewell. While Fred was never estranged from his mother and father, the person he always depended on and found stability in was his sister, Jewell.

Above: Fred Wilkerson, circa 1941.
Courtesy of Tim Wilkerson.

Right: Fred Wilkerson, circa 1945.
Courtesy of Tim Wilkerson.

Left: Fred Wilkerson, age twelve, 1950. *Right*: Fred Wilkerson Heard's County High School senior picture. *Courtesy of Tim Wilkerson.*

The Wilkerson kids knew that there wasn't much prospect for a future there on the rocky red clay hills of Randolph County, Alabama. Jewell became enamored of a young neighbor boy named Durrell Sanders, who was a year her junior. Jewell had left high school in her junior year, but Durrell went on to graduate from Heard County High School, and in 1950, they were married and moved to LaGrange, Georgia, just a few miles down the road. Durrell knew the prospects for employment and his family's future would be better there. He began work at Piston Ring and Supply. It was the largest auto parts dealer in the LaGrange area. He would spend his working life in the auto parts business.

Young Fred remained in close contact with his beloved sister and Durrell, as they were only twenty miles away. While Fred remained tied to the family farm throughout his high school years, he spent as much time as he could with Jewell and Durrell. The Sanderses loved Fred and welcomed any time they had with him.

Durrell and Jewell welcomed their first child, Sharon, in February 1952. A second baby girl, Jane, followed in June 1956. Fred assumed more of an older brother role with the girls, even though he was their uncle. Soon after Fred

Above: Fred, Zelmer, Alma and Jewell. *Courtesy of Tim Wilkerson.*

Left: Fred and Jewell. *Courtesy of Tim Wilkerson.*

graduated high school in May 1958, he left the Alabama homestead and moved in with the Sanders family in LaGrange. Fred knew that there was little opportunity for employment—much less building a career—around the old farm. Durrell and Jewell welcomed him with open arms into their family. Once again, Fred assumed the role of son more than a brother to the Sanderses. According to sisters Sharon and Jane, that suited them just fine. Fred became the full-time brother they'd never had.

After moving in with the Sanderses, Fred found a job with the Hav-A-Tampa Cigar and Candy Company as a route salesman, servicing stores in the LaGrange area. One of the stores he serviced happened to be close to where he lived with the Sanderses. It was called Yellow Jacket Service Station, named for the creek that ran close by. It was owned and operated by Jack Lee. Jack had a daughter, Carolyn. It was Carolyn who caught Fred's eye, and a romance between them blossomed. They were married on May 1, 1961. Their first child, a girl named Tracie, was born on November 10, 1964, followed four years later by their second child, a boy named Tim, who was born on November 2, 1968. Like everyone else, their marriage wasn't perfect, but for twenty-one of their twenty-two years together, they made it work. They raised a family in a loving and caring environment, and according to his children, Fred was everything a father should be—until Connie Quedens made her way into their lives.

Fred, having been raised in a matriarchal situation, hated conflict and controversy, especially with women, and he would do most anything he could to avoid it, often to his detriment. It was this Achilles heel, years later, that fatally entangled him in the black widow's web.

THE BLACK WIDOW

Connie King was born on March 22, 1945, in Clay County, West Virginia, into a life of abject poverty. She was the daughter of Wert Hansford King and Ora Marcelle Dobinsbrook King. Wert was a West Virginia coal miner. Life in Appalachia was worse than hard—it was brutal. The family struggled to eke out a living on the meager wages Wert earned shoveling coal in the Elk River Coal Mine in Widen, West Virginia. Conditions for the Kings were deplorable. Their house was little more than a shack with no running water. They ate either what they could raise on the mountainous hills of Clay County or what they could get from the company store of the Elk River Mining Company, to which the miners were kept in constant debt. The children's clothes were mostly homemade hand-me-downs. Shoes came only in the bitter mountain winters. It was everything the horrors of life in the region known as Appalachia was billed to be. It was one of the poorest regions in America in the 1940s and '50s.

Connie King experienced a harsh childhood. Like so many others in the region, she never enjoyed the amenities afforded to those from less impoverished areas. This likely explains why she became so possessed by the need to have control and the overwhelming desire for material things. As Connie grew into her teenage years, the one thing she became sure of was that she was willing to do whatever was necessary to put the coal dust of Clay County, West Virginia, and the life she had lived there behind her.

She discovered a possible vehicle for her ambitions when she met Gary Quedens, an engineering student at the University of West Virginia. Gary was intelligent, ambitious and not afraid to work. He was putting himself through school, handling freight at a local trucking terminal. Gary was not an exceptionally worldly young man, but Connie saw him as her ticket out of coal country. Connie and Gary were married on April 6, 1963, in Spencer, West Virginia.

Gary graduated with a degree in industrial engineering and found employment as a plant engineer and began to establish a career for himself. Gary had a love for fast cars and racing, and he befriended a local mechanic and fellow racing enthusiast named Bob Hulderman. Bob's wife, Joan, would later lament that Connie made every effort to inject herself into their personal lives and would attempt to spend as much time as she could around Bob when Joan was not around. Joan went on to say that Bob always said he knew what Connie was about and that he always tried to not be put in a position to ruin his friendship with Gary. Connie began to attend a local community college and got a job with the city of Fairmont, West Virginia. It didn't take long for Connie's wandering eye to home in on a local lawyer named James Esposito. In 1985, Esposito was found guilty in federal court on racketeering and narcotics charges, resulting from a 1983 indictment under the RICO Statute, along with seventeen others who had conspired to import large amounts of cocaine through Miami to be distributed in the Northeast.

Connie's first brush with the law came in 1978, when she was employed as a bookkeeper and clerk with the City of Fairmont. She was accused of felony theft from her employer after ordering sets of tires, billing them to the Water and Sewer Board and converting them to her own use. In May 1980, Connie pleaded guilty to the charge and was sentenced to one to five years in the custody of the West Virginia Department of Corrections. That sentence was suspended upon restitution and her successful completion of two years of supervised probation.

In 1983, Gary Quedens accepted a position at Freudenberg-NOK, a manufacturing concern in LaGrange, Georgia, as an industrial engineer. This brought the Quedens family to LaGrange, where they purchased a home in the affluent subdivision of Eagles Rest on West Point Lake. Gary thought this was his family's chance to start anew. Connie, on the other hand, would use this opportunity to entrap others in the black widow's web.

THE SAVIOR SYNDROME

S ome people have an intense desire to help others or to try to improve others' situations in life, many times to their own detriment. This is common in people who involve themselves in community causes. This behavior is especially prevalent among people associated with the public safety field.

Fred Wilkerson was a person who, by all accounts, would give you the shirt off his back. Fred was the chief of the Troup County Ware's Cross Road Volunteer Fire Department; he coached his son Tim's Little League Baseball team; and according to everyone close to him, if you needed help, Fred was just a phone call away.

Carolyn Wilkerson was a strong-willed, independent woman. The one thing Carolyn didn't need was saving. She was totally devoted to her family; she and Fred raised their children in what could be described as a very average working-class family. Carolyn worked as the office manager for Jack Davis Concrete in LaGrange. She didn't place a lot of demands on Fred in the marriage. He was a good provider, a good father and, until the arrival of Connie Quedens, a good husband.

By all accounts, life was good at the Wilkerson house until shortly after Connie Quedens came to work in the office at Gusto Brands, a local beverage distributor in LaGrange, in June 1983. Fred was a longtime employee and the warehouse manager there.

It wasn't long before Connie found a listening ear in Fred; she told him continual tales of her mistreatment and neglect at the hands of her husband.

Fred Wilkerson at a family gathering in 1985. *Courtesy of Tim Wilkerson.*

Fred Wilkerson standing beside a tractor. *Courtesy of Tim Wilkerson.*

Fred Wilkerson with his family. *Courtesy of Tim Wilkerson.*

Fred Wilkerson enjoying a day at the beach. *Courtesy of Tim Wilkerson.*

Over the next several months, their relationship grew in the direction Connie steered it. Connie used Fred's personality and character to ensnare him in a relationship that would eventually cost him everything.

It appeared to begin innocently enough, with Connie requesting him to come to her home to do yard work and handyman tasks that she couldn't get her husband to complete. She always had some type of crisis for which she would inevitably request Fred's help to resolve. In true Fred fashion, he always came to the rescue. Fred could not say no. Connie made the impression that she was in constant peril, when in fact, she was constantly as she had always been: conjuring some scheme driven by greed and lust for control. Incident by incident, she was spinning the strands of the web that would ensnare Fred Wilkerson.

RESURRECTION BY STORM

In life, some things just can't be simply explained; events and situations arise that most people regard as products of happenstance or just plain luck. I, for one, think that sometimes greater powers are in play. I believe that God works in mysterious ways and in his own time.

By the summer of 2003, Fred Wilkerson had been missing for almost eighteen years. Only those closest to Fred, his family and friends, had kept his memory alive and were still haunted by the pain they had suffered for so long. Law enforcement had all but closed the book on Fred's case, and it became just another cold missing person case.

His children, Tim and Tracie, had long resigned themselves to the fact that they would never have the answers they had so long sought about what had happened to their father. After all the years of asking questions, posting hundreds of flyers and begging for answers, they had never come any closer than another false sighting of their father leading to yet another dead end. As a matter of self-preservation, they had finally found the resolve to move on with their lives with only the memories of their father to cleave to.

Like most summers in Georgia, the summer of 2003 had been oppressively hot, but the afternoon thunderstorms were unseasonably violent. One late August evening, a particularly strong storm blew in from the west with high winds and torrential rain. The storm brought widespread damage to Troup County; trees were blown down, power was lost, homes and businesses were damaged. As awful as the storm was, looking back, I know in my heart that it was an act of divine intervention.

The storm set into motion a chain of inexplicable events—events that would prove to be life-changing for the loved ones of Fred Wilkerson, God-given circumstances that would lead to long-overdue justice for Fred Wilkerson and his family.

Those violent winds of change snapped huge Georgia pines like toothpicks, and it just so happened that one of those great trees landed squarely on the brand-new, fire engine–red pickup truck that belonged to my boss, Coweta Circuit district attorney Pete Skandalakis, crushing it.

The next morning, Pete came into the office with that look of having lost his last friend and told the story of how his new prized possession had been reduced to a pickup pancake. After I spent a few minutes trying to console my friend on his loss, the conversation got around to which shop would be the best to attend to the problem. I told Pete that I would take his truck to West Georgia Paint and Body, a shop well known for its quality work that was owned by Tim Wilkerson.

After a quick call to Tim to be sure he could take a look at the truck to determine if it indeed was fixable or a total loss, we set out to see if we could get the truck to the shop. Upon our arrival at Pete's house, the situation was not pretty. Workers had removed the tree, but the roof of the truck was caved in, all the windows and the windshield were broken out and the bed was also crushed. The truck, however, did crank and seemed to be somewhat mobile, much to our surprise. The damage was extreme, but we decided we'd try to get the now convertible to the shop. We swept the glass out of the seat; I crawled in the somewhat restricted space beneath the crushed roof, and with Pete in tow, I was off.

After our somewhat comical journey, we arrived at Tim's shop. We spoke with Tim, and he agreed to handle the situation with Pete's insurance company. Just in conversation, Tim said he had heard that we had made an arrest in a thirty-three-year-old cold case and offered his congratulations. He went on to say that he wished that there was a chance that his dad's case could be reviewed, as he knew of some leads that he thought had never been followed up on. I looked at Pete and asked if I could review the case, and he said of course and that we'd be glad to give it another look. I think

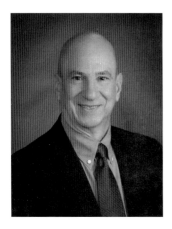

Peter "Pete" John Skandalakis, district attorney, Coweta Judicial Circuit. *Courtesy of Peter John Skandalakis.*

Tim made the request out of a sense of duty to his father, but I could see the feeling of futility in his eyes as he spoke of his father's case. I told Tim I'd be in touch in a day or so to gather some information; with that, Tim thanked us, and we were on our way.

After we left West Georgia Paint and Body, Pete and I talked about Tim's request. I told Pete I was surprised to hear Tim disappointedly mention leads that he felt had been ignored. I couldn't imagine that there had been any significant information that had not been followed up on.

One thing was for sure: if there was validity to his sense that some stones had been left unturned, I was going to try my best to roll them over to see what might be underneath. I could not imagine being in Tim's situation, seeking answers all those years while never believing that my father had abandoned his family.

Little did we know, this was just the beginning of the unraveling of the black widow's web.

A STARTING POINT

The day after Pete and I had our initial conversation with Tim, I contacted him to schedule a meeting. Tim said he and his sister, Tracie, had a compilation of records and notes that he felt would be beneficial for me to have. He suggested that he get those together and meet me at his office the following day. I agreed that the sooner we meet the better, and I said I would see him the next morning at 9:00 a.m.

When I arrived at Tim's shop the next morning, I was filled with a resolve and determination to do all I could to relieve the suffering of this family. They had been through so much for so long. They deserved some answers, and I was going to do everything I could to try to help them find them.

Tim met me in the front lobby, and we went back into his office. As he spoke about the case and his father, I could feel the pain in his voice. He said that he, his sister and his father had remained extremely close, even after his parents divorced. He stated flatly, "There is no way my dad just up and left us without a word. He never missed my ball games, Tracie's recitals—anything we had, he was always there for us. He wasn't just my dad, he was my best friend."

I was not familiar with the case at all and knew very little about those involved. That was about to change dramatically. In a case where a person disappears under suspicious circumstances and without a trace, an investigator must acquire as much intimate knowledge as they can of the lives of those involved to determine a starting point for his quest for the truth.

We spoke about the case in general and about the things that were going on in his life before his dad's disappearance. The one thing that was abundantly clear was that Fred's family attributed his downward spiral and disappearance to his relationship with Connie Quedens. Tim gave me a list of some of Fred's close friends, employers and associates so that I might get to know Fred Wilkerson further.

Tim was then supposed to meet with his sister, and together, they were going to get all the records they had and provide me with a timeline of events leading up to the disappearance of their father. We agreed to meet again the following afternoon at Tim's home.

After this meeting with Tim, I immediately began contacting the people who Tim said his dad had been close to so that I might judge for myself the possibility that Fred may have abandoned his life. One of those people was Raymon Vaughan. Raymon and his wife, Jerrell, were close friends of Fred and Carolyn Wilkerson as young married couples raising their children; they often spent hours in the evenings playing cards and watching their children play together. I knew Raymon to be a very frank and straightforward man. When asked his opinion about what happened to Fred, he said flatly that Fred Wilkerson hadn't just up and left; Fred was too close to his kids to have done that. Raymon, who knew the story of Fred and Connie, said, "You don't have to look no further than her to find out what happened to Fred."

I told Raymon that I had been given the go-ahead to reopen the case and that I intended to get to the truth of what happened to his friend. Raymon looked at me, chuckled and said, "Hell, boy, I hope you do, but I doubt that you're gonna get any closer to what happened to Fred than the rest of them did." At that point, I had to say I agreed with Raymon on my chances, but just like my dad always said, "Son, you'll miss every shot you never take." I knew in my heart that Fred and his family deserved one more shot.

WHAT YOU NEED TO KNOW

Most crimes start off with an act, a victim, a crime scene and, hopefully, evidence and suspects. In Fred Wilkerson's case, most of those elements were missing. All there was was the fact that Fred was missing. At that point, sometimes the best thing to do is to listen—listen to the people who knew him, his character, the things that made him Fred.

All too often, we look for reasons to not inquire, hoping things will all work out. It's the easy path to take. Any inquiry into Fred's personality, character, work history and, above all, relationship with his children, would have raised tremendous doubt that Fred, after having Thanksgiving dinner with his family and being prepared to go to work the next morning, would simply ride off into the sunset, never to be heard from again. To me, considering the situation, that thought was absurd.

After talking to members of his family, coworkers, employers and friends, I concluded that there was no way in hell Fred Wilkerson had abandoned his family, leaving them to suffer the torture of living with the unknown.

I spoke to a number of people who were intimately involved in Fred Wilkerson's life, and not one of those people believed Fred had elected to just walk away from his life to start anew. The people who knew Fred best were adamant that he would never have walked away from his family. In his marriage to Carolyn, Fred might not have been the best husband, but no one could deny that he was an excellent father.

This page: Fred Wilkerson with his children, Tim and Tracie. *Courtesy of Tim Wilkerson.*

If, in fact, Fred had not abandoned his life, one would have to assume he had met some unfortunate circumstance. The consensus of everyone who knew Fred and were familiar with his situation with Connie Quedens was that she had something to do with his disappearance.

Connie had been asked for an interview early on in the investigation, and on December 1, 1987, she met with investigators at the Troup County Sheriff's Office, accompanied by her attorney Jack Kirby. At the time, she was asked to take a polygraph test but flatly refused, and then she was questioned about her financial involvement with Fred and the details of their relationship. She stated there was no romantic relationship between her and Fred, although he and his son had lived in the same house with her for several months before she demanded they leave on Labor Day 1987.

According to Tim Wilkerson, his father lived upstairs with Connie while he resided in the basement. It was apparent that there had been a romantic relationship between Fred and Connie for a long period. Fred intended for the home he had built at 421 Ware's Crossroad to become his and Connie's marital residence.

From 1984 until just before Fred disappeared, Fred would bring Connie to family gatherings and so forth. Everyone was under the impression that they were, in fact, a couple with long-term aspirations and that Fred was doing all he could to prepare for a life with Connie. According to those closest to Fred, the more Connie demanded, the more Fred was willing to sell his soul to please her. It was a weakness in his character that Connie learned she could exploit to the fullest. Fred could not say no to her incessant demands. It was his inability to resist her iron will that would lead to his hopeless entanglement in the black widow's web.

GREAT REVELATIONS

Tim and Tracie had gotten right to work on getting together the things that I had asked for. Over the years, Tracie had compiled a large volume of records pertaining to Fred's disappearance, as well as a complete paper trail that chronicled the financial entanglement that Fred had been enticed into by Connie.

The siblings produced records dating from 1983 until Fred's disappearance. They contained every real estate transaction in which Connie and Fred were entwined. They also had photographs of Connie and Fred at Wilkerson family gatherings in which it was evident that Fred was much more than the yard man Connie had claimed. They had detailed records of the progression of the construction of the house, expenditures, names of subcontractors and material vendors as well. While all this could have related to a motive for Connie to want Fred dead, there was no direct evidence that linked her to his disappearance. Tim and Tracie mentioned several instances of being told that the investigation was being reopened, but each time, the results were the same: no one followed up on their leads. They said they felt abandoned and left to suffer the unknown without any support.

As we spoke, I was told of other people, subsequent to Connie's involvement with Fred, who had also had serious conflicts with Connie. There were incidents in which Connie exhibited violent behavior toward those who refused to buckle under her demands.

They then told me of an incident that I thought should surely have led to a break in the case. Their attorney Peter Alford had told them of a revelation that had taken place in 1995, shortly after the probate action was filed by Connie to have Fred declared dead. Peter had been contacted by Lisa Hulderman Miles, who had information that could possibly lead to a bombshell break in the case. Alford had called and reported the information to the authorities, but it had apparently led nowhere.

I felt there had to be more to the story, because surely to God, information of this magnitude had been followed up on. But apparently it hadn't been. I couldn't understand why no one had reported their findings, positive or negative, to either Tim and Tracie or Peter Alford.

I left Tim's house feeling like a man on fire. I was confident that we were heading down a path that might very well lead to justice for Fred and those who loved him.

I knew that I had to substantiate with Peter Alford the story I had been given. I contacted Peter and asked him to come to my office to discuss this and another old case that I had been asked to look into. Upon his arrival, Peter, whom I had known for a long time, began to relate the events of the probate action and the resulting call from Lisa Hulderman. I knew I had to find out if her story had changed and, if not, why it had never resulted in any progress in the case. As it turned out, Pete Alford's long-neglected information would be the key to unlocking the secrets of the black widow's web.

10

STRANDS OF THE WEB

In order to understand how something as delicate as a spider's web can hopelessly entrap victims that appear much larger and stronger than the web, one needs to examine the strands from which it is made. Connie Quedens spent a lifetime spinning those stands. It began long before Fred Wilkerson and continued until long after he was gone.

Fred had been employed at Gusto Brands since 1973; the company had seen his work ethic and dedication to his job, and he had advanced into management to the position of warehouse manager, a challenging role of responsibility requiring trust.

In the summer of 1983, Connie Quedens took a job at Gusto as a clerk/bookkeeper. In September that year, according to Fred's children, Connie began calling Fred's home with requests for assistance at her home. Tim recollected his first time going to the Quedenses' house with his dad. Connie had called and said she had seen a snake in the woodpile behind the house, and Tim remembered going over there with his dad to search for a snake they didn't find. That was only the beginning. The requests became more frequent until Fred left home after twenty-two years of marriage and moved into the Versailles Apartments with Tracie's fiancé, Roger Campbell. Connie visited there often.

In December 1983, Carolyn filed for divorce, which would become final in February 1984.

Fred moved into Commerce Court Apartments in December 1983, and Connie was seen there regularly. In December 1984, Fred bought a small house at 1360 Youngs Mill Road. Connie gave Fred money for the down payment to make the purchase. In March 1985, Fred bought three acres of land adjoining the house on Youngs Mill Road.

In April 1985, Connie called Fred and told him Gary had discovered that she had given him the down payment for the Youngs Mill property. Connie convinced Gary that she had, in fact, loaned Fred the money and that he had made no effort to repay the debt. She said Gary was demanding that she sue him in state court for the return of the money. The suit was filed by Gary and Connie. They received a $6,600 judgment. Fred sold the house on Youngs Mill Road to his future son-in-law, Roger Campbell. Roger gave the Quedenses $4,500, along with a motorcycle, as a down payment.

Connie also demanded Fred take out a $20,000 term life insurance policy with her as the beneficiary. In mid-1985, Connie was terminated at Gusto Brands for undisclosed reasons. She then went to work at the LaGrange Honda dealership owned by Clarence Fincher as an office manager and bookkeeper.

In May 1985, Fred bought a mobile home and placed it on the Youngs Mill property he had previously purchased. Fred and Connie continued their relationship. According to family members, Connie was often there at the mobile home with her car hidden in the back and sometimes covered with a tarp.

In October 1985, Connie filed for divorce from Gary. There would be no further action taken on the divorce until just before Fred's disappearance in 1987.

In April 1986, Fred purchased fourteen and a half acres of land on Wares Crossroad with the intention of building a house that would serve as his and Connie's marital residence.

Fred conveyed half interest in the land to Connie in October 1986, and the deed stated that it was conveyed for "love and affection." Together, they obtained a construction loan from First Federal Savings and Loan in the amount of $89,000 to build the house.

In October 1986, Connie demanded Fred quit his job at Gusto Brands and seek employment that would pay him better. Fred did so and went to work as a driver for Fast Food Merchandisers, a food distribution company that serves fast food restaurants in the Southeast.

Then in July 1986, Fred made a will that, in the event of his death, bequeathed all his property to Connie.

Fred obtained a contractor's license in February 1987 to comply with code regulations to finish the house at 421 Wares Crossroad, and then a month later, Fred moved into the house while he was still working to complete the construction. Connie wanted Fred to build a pool at the house. In the spring of 1987, Fred attempted to borrow $10,000 to build the pool, but he was overextended and First Federal required him to obtain a cosigner. Don Rainey, a close friend of Fred, signed the note with him.

Tim moved into the house with Fred, as did Connie and her two boys, Garrett and Guerin, in early May 1987. Connie convinced Fred that having the other half of the land in her name solely would help her retain custody of her boys in her pending divorce that had lain fallow since 1985. According to family members, Connie promised to deed the land back when the divorce was finalized and she and Fred were married. On May 8, 1987, Fred deeded the other half of the land to Connie, and she then owned the property in total.

On May 22, 1987, Connie applied for a permanent mortgage loan to repay the construction loan in the amount of $123,000 in her name only. Her debt to earnings ratio exceeded her credit, and in true Connie fashion, she convinced her employer Clarence Fincher to cosign the note with her, making her the sole owner of the house that Fred built, along with all the property. Fincher had just recently lost his wife of fifty years, and Connie found him to be an easy mark.

Connie amended her divorce with Gary on July 2, 1987, and it became final on August 10, 1987.

On Labor Day weekend 1987, Connie started an argument with Tim. Connie called the sheriff's office, unknown to Fred, and had him and Tim arrested for criminal trespassing and removed from the property. After Fred posted bond, he was allowed to return, escorted by a deputy, to retrieve his and Tim's personal belongings, but he had instructions not to return. Gary Quedens moved into the house the next day.

Fred and Tim moved into a duplex at 116 Northwoods Drive on September 8, 1987. They were living there on November 23, 1987, when the bank called in the loan for the $10,000 that Fred had borrowed with Don Rainey as a cosigner. Fred did not have the means to repay the loan at the time, so Don had to repay it. Don had seen the entire saga with Fred and Connie, and he was convinced that Fred had been duped from the start. He told Fred that in order for their friendship to survive, he needed to meet with attorney H.J. Thomas to see if there was any avenue for Fred to recoup some of the money that he had been conned out of. Thomas, after hearing the story, felt that there might be an actionable cause.

H.J. Thomas filed a lawsuit on Fred's behalf on November 24, 1987, in the amount of $37,071.21. This sum included $23,000, the initial cost of the fourteen and a half acres of land; the $10,000 Fred had borrowed for the pool; and the amount Fred had spent out of pocket on materials and supplies that could be verified.

Connie Quedens was served with the lawsuit on Tuesday, November 25, 1987, two days before Thanksgiving. Connie called Fred and proceeded in a profanity-laced tirade to ask what he thought he was doing and why he had filed the suit. In true Fred fashion, his only reply was an apologetic "I had to."

Connie and Gary had made plans to visit relatives in Port Richey, Florida, over the Thanksgiving weekend. They were to leave on Wednesday, and arrangements had been made with Joan Hulderman to take care of their animals. On Wednesday, November 26, 1987, Connie called Joan Hulderman and stated she was not going to make the trip with Gary and the boys. When asked why she wasn't going, according to Joan Hulderman, Connie's response was, "I have to stay to protect my property." Early in the investigation, no one spoke with the Huldermans, even though they were arguably those closest to the Quedenses and Fred Wilkerson. Later on, this would prove to be a haunting omission.

On November 27, 1987, Thanksgiving Day, Fred attended family Thanksgiving dinner at his sister, Jewell's, home along with both his children, Tim and Tracie, and other family and friends. Fred left, saying he had to get some rest before he and Tim left early the next morning on their trip to Tennessee. Fred was awakened around 11:00 p.m. by Tiffany Roberts, who was looking for her boyfriend, who was out with Tim. She was reportedly the last person to see Fred Wilkerson. Sometime after she left, Fred got a call from Connie, demanding that he come over to discuss the lawsuit. When Tim arrived home around 1:00 a.m., his father was gone, though his clothes and shaving bag, packed for the next day's trip, were laid out on the bed. Fred Wilkerson was never heard from again.

On December 24, 1987, Fred's champagne-colored 1987 Honda was located in long-term parking at Hartfield-Jackson Airport in Atlanta. It was taken into evidence and processed by a Georgia Bureau of Investigation evidence technician who stated the car had been wiped clean and that no identifiable fingerprints could be found. Inside, a few pieces of personal property, along with two uncashed payroll checks made out to Fred Wilkerson, were found.

This would conclude the long and convoluted history between Connie King Quedens and Willie Fred Wilkerson. It would lead to many more questions than answers, and unfortunately, those answers would not come for a long time.

11

SPOTS ON THE LEOPARD

Despite their efforts early on, law enforcement just could not get any traction in pursuing Fred Wilkerson's case as anything other than a missing persons case. While an aura of suspicion was on Connie Quedens, there was no direct evidence to connect her with Fred's disappearance. Every time Connie spoke to authorities, she had her attorney present, and she always had a good attorney who would advise her to say basically nothing—which she did.

As time wore on, Connie refused any further attempts to cooperate with the authorities—to the point of threatening legal action if they persisted. It was basically "charge me or don't bother me." With what they had, law enforcement was at an impasse.

However, in 1995, greed once again reared its ugly head, as Connie filed an action in probate court to have Fred, who had now been missing for seven years, declared dead and herself placed as executor of his estate, based on the fact that she was holding two term life insurance policies on Fred's life. Clearly, she was an interested party in the distribution of his estate. As my dad always said, the spots on the leopard never change. Connie was a true narcissist; until this point, everything in this case had emboldened her. For seven years, she had been able to fend off law enforcement at every turn. She felt absolutely bulletproof and was comfortable enacting what would become the next and final step in what was apparently her long-term plan.

The Wilkerson family objected, of course, and hired local attorney Peter Alford to defend their position in a protracted probate hearing. It was during this hearing that Alford revisited the missing persons case and exposed much of the financial and personal relationship between Fred and Connie. He also went into great detail with other facts involved in the case, elaborating on Fred's disappearance on Thanksgiving 1987 and the discovery of his car on Christmas Eve 1987 at Hartsfield-Jackson Airport in Atlanta, which was the first evidence found in the case.

Alford contacted Joel Martin of the *LaGrange Daily News*, and due to the notoriety of the case, Martin covered the proceedings extensively. In a negotiated settlement, Quedens was allowed to collect $10,000 on the term life policy on which she had been paying the premiums semiannually since Fred's disappearance. The premiums on the $20,000 policy that Connie demanded Fred take out in 1985 were being debited from Fred's checking account until the account became overdrawn in September 1989 and the policy lapsed. Despite their best efforts, the Quedenses were unable to collect on that policy.

Shortly after the probate hearing, Peter Alford received a phone call from a young woman who identified herself as Lisa Hulderman Miles. She stated that she had information regarding the Wilkerson case. Miles informed Alford that in 1987, on Thanksgiving weekend, Connie Quedens had asked her to pick her up at the Atlanta airport. She went on to tell Alford that she had been friends with the Wilkersons and the Quedenses and that it was not uncommon for Connie to call on her and other members of her family for help. She stated that, at the time, she was just a teenager and had never been aware that Fred's car was later found at the airport until she had seen the account in the paper while visiting her mother.

Realizing the value of this information to the case, Alford notified the investigator in charge of the case at the time, Kenneth Reed of the Troup County Sheriff's Office, by phone. He also followed up with a letter to the sheriff's office and advised the Wilkerson family of the information given by Lisa Miles.

Thinking this might be game-changing information, the Wilkerson family anxiously waited to hear some news—and waited and waited. After some time, Peter, Tim and Tracie just assumed that this information had led to another crushing dead end. With the apparent value of the information, they felt sure it would have been followed up on to some conclusion.

Once again, they were disappointed.

I can't say why this information was ignored. I feel sure if it had been conveyed to the GBI agent who was working the case, it would have resulted in a resolution to the case. Not only was the ball dropped, but it was also fumbled off the playing field.

In the end, it was Peter Alford's long-ignored revelation that would breathe life back into the case of the disappearance of Fred Wilkerson and revive the effort to unravel the black widow's web.

12

NOSE TO THE GROUND

You can always pick out a good dog; when it's time to hunt, he has his nose to the ground. It was time for me to get my nose on the ground.

With the revelation from Lisa being verified by Peter Alford, I needed to find Lisa Hulderman, now Miles, as quickly as possible. I did know that her father, Bob Hulderman, was working at Lukken Chevrolet, just as he had been for the past twenty years. On September 4, 2003, I went there and found Bob. When I asked him about the events with Connie, he said he had always suspected that Connie was responsible for Fred's disappearance. He went on to say that because of the relationship his family had with the Quedenses and Fred, he had always expected someone to come to inquire about their knowledge of the situation, but no one ever had.

He said that when Lisa had seen the newspaper article and called the Wilkersons' lawyer about the trip to the airport, they were sure that someone was going to talk to her about what she had done. Then again, no one came or called.

I told Bob that, at that point, I wasn't sure why that had happened, but I needed to talk to Lisa as soon as I could, as the case was reopened and I was searching for answers. Bob told me Lisa had gotten married and was living in Goose Creek, South Carolina, near Charleston. He also gave me her phone number.

I went back to my office and immediately called Lisa. She was somewhat astounded that I was reaching out to her. I told her that I was investigating Fred Wilkerson's disappearance and had just been informed of the call she made to Peter Alford in 1995.

Lisa acknowledged that she had, in fact, contacted Alford after seeing the article in the paper describing the discovery of Fred's car at the airport. She felt her information would surely be valuable in solving the case and was mystified when no one ever contacted her to follow up on her story.

I asked her if she would meet with me the following day at a place of her choosing to get a written statement of the events as they had transpired. Lisa asked if it would be possible to meet at Patch Insurance Agency, her place of employment in Charleston. She said she would be there at 9:00 a.m. I told her that I would be there at that time.

I immediately went to Pete with what I had discovered and told him I needed to go to Charleston the next day. Pete seemed just as excited by the news as I had been and told me to carry on with whatever I needed to do.

After giving it a bit of thought, I contacted Tim Wilkerson and told him of my progress and plans. He had been disappointed so many times that he was somewhat skeptical yet hopeful that we might indeed be making some progress in the case. He wished me good luck on my trip.

I left for Charleston at four o'clock the next morning to begin what would be a whirlwind of activity over the next few weeks as I set about tearing away at the strands of the black widow's web.

13

AN ENLIGHTENING CONVERSATION

I was in the parking lot at Patch Insurance Agency in Charleston when Lisa arrived for work just before 9:00 a.m. I introduced myself and told her how much I appreciated her being willing to meet with me. She invited me into her office, and we began to talk about what she experienced. We spoke in general about how she knew the Quedenses.

She said that her father, Bob Hulderman, had become friends with Gary Quedens through their common interest in race cars. Bob actually did mechanic work on a car that Gary owned while they all lived in West Virginia.

She went on to say that the Quedenses had moved to LaGrange, Georgia, and that, shortly after, her father was contacted by Gary, who said there was a job opportunity in LaGrange. Gary offered to help find them a place and get settled. The economy was in the tank in West Virginia, and it was a struggle for the Hulderman family, so Bob agreed to move them to LaGrange.

Upon arriving in LaGrange, Bob learned that the job was working at a shop called Oak Automotive. It was owned by Otto Korth, who had met the Quedenses through church. Connie was working in the office there, and Bob stayed only a short while before going to work for Lukken Chevrolet. The Huldermans remained friends with the Quedenses mostly because of the relationship between Gary and Bob. The Huldermans' home was not far from the Quedenses', and according to Lisa and other members of the family, Connie would often call on them to help with chores and different tasks around their home. This continued and even increased when Connie moved into the house on Ware's Cross Road.

Lisa, who had just graduated from high school at the time, stated that on the Friday after Thanksgiving 1987, she worked the night shift at the Florence Hand Nursing Home in LaGrange. When she got off Saturday morning, her sister Shelly was on the phone with Connie Quedens, who had asked her if she could drive a car to the Atlanta airport. Shelly told her she could not but that Lisa had just come in and she might be able to. Lisa spoke with Connie and agreed to come help her.

When she arrived at Connie's home, she was met in the driveway by Connie, who told her that she had a friend who was visiting from West Virginia and that she had a rental car. She went on to say that the friend had too much to drink and that she was going to drive her rental car to the airport to turn it and needed to be picked up. Lisa thought it strange that when she asked where the friend was, Connie said she'd gone to get gas, even though she'd just told her she had been drinking too much to drive. Lisa said it was also strange that when she got there, Connie's car was sitting in the driveway with the garage door closed, which it never was.

Lisa said Connie gave her explicit instructions to take her car back through LaGrange to get on the interstate, which was also strange, as it added about thirty minutes to the trip, but she did as she was told. She drove directly to the interstate and drove the speed limit the entire way. Connie also instructed her to pick her up in front of the terminal instead of the car rental area. She drove away with Connie standing in the driveway.

Lisa had assumed that Connie was going to take her friend to a hotel, but to her amazement, upon her arrival at the airport, Connie was already standing in front of the terminal. When Lisa inquired about her friend and how quickly she had gotten her to the hotel, Connie was very evasive, never really addressing the question. They then drove directly back to Connie's, and when they arrived, the garage door was up and the garage was empty. They drove right into the garage and parked. Lisa then left and went home.

Lisa said, at first, she heard nothing about Fred—not until she learned he was missing a few days later. She never knew Fred's car was discovered at the airport until the newspaper article recounting the events was released during the probate action in 1995. Lisa said she immediately put the events together and was sure Connie had taken Fred's car to the airport. She went on to say that shortly after the events at the airport, Connie hired Lisa and her sisters to come and drag brush in an effort to fill in an old well on the property. After the well was filled in, Connie tried to set fire to the brush in the well, but it only smoldered and didn't burn. Lisa went on to say that Connie, at some point, had a man with equipment fill in the well. Lisa said she believed Connie killed Fred and put his body in the old well.

The article outlining the information uncovered during the probate proceedings identified Peter Alford as representing the Wilkersons. Lisa said she felt she had to let someone know about these events, so she got Alford's number, called him and told him the same story she told me. She said she just knew any day someone would contact her, but they never did. Lisa said she and her family were scared of Connie because they knew of her volatile personality and had seen her exhibit outbursts of anger. We talked a bit longer; I told her I wasn't sure why her information hadn't been followed up on, but I assured her that I felt it was going to play an instrumental role in finding justice for Fred and his family. I knew that this would be the key to taking down the black widow's web.

14

YOU GOTTA DIG A LITTLE DEEPER IN THE WELL

It was late when I got back from Charleston, but the next morning, I was in Pete's office, bringing him up to speed on the events of the day before. He was elated at the progress I had made. I told him I was sure we would be able to bring this case to a successful conclusion. Pete then said we would have to get with the sheriff's office to let them know of our progress on the case and get them involved. I agreed and called Sheriff Donny Turner, and I asked to meet with him and Captain Willis Grizzard. We met later that day, and I advised them of all that had transpired. I told them that I was going to follow up on locating where the well had been on the property, and at that point, I said we should seek a search warrant for the Quedenses' property at 421 Ware's Crossroad. Captain Grizzard agreed that would be the best path to follow.

I again contacted Bob Hulderman to get any information I could on the Quedenses' current situation and to ask if, by chance, he knew the exact location of the old well on the property. He said he still maintained contact with Gary Quedens and that Gary and Connie were once again in the middle of a divorce. Bob said that when Connie filed for divorce, Gary actually stayed with the Huldermans until Connie and the boys moved out of the house in Eagle's Rest. Bob went on to say that he had no contact with Connie and that he didn't like the way she treated people. He indicated he had gotten angry with her when he found out she had involved his daughters in the incident Lisa reported in 1995 and that he had avoided her ever since.

When I asked Bob about the well, he said he knew its general location and that Connie had actually called him around the time Fred disappeared to tell him that if he needed to dispose of anything—even old appliances—he could put it in the well, as she was trying to get it filled. She told Bob it was a hazard and presented a dangerous situation for the children. He went on to say that Connie, at one time, had Jessie Patterson do work at her house with a Bobcat. I thought that if, on the off chance, that work included filling in a well, I needed to talk to Jessie Patterson.

Jessie was one of the people who I had been told had some difficulties with Connie. When I left Bob Hulderman, I headed straight to the Hillcrest Road home of Jessie Patterson. I knew Jessie; he was a retired U.S. Army master sergeant with thirty years of service. I had spoken with him often when our paths crossed through the years. As luck would have it, as I passed the Hillcrest Bait and Tackle Grocery convenience store, I saw Jessie at the gas pumps. I pulled in and asked if he had a minute to talk to me. He said, "Sure, what you got up, Mr. Bryant?" I had always told Jessie my father was Mr. Bryant and for him just to call me Clay. I guess the habit came from his long stint in the army, but he always respectfully addressed other men as "mister." I told him I was investigating the old Fred Wilkerson case and had been told that he'd had some dealings with Connie Quedens. He said he regretfully had. He said that after he retired in 1989 and returned to LaGrange, his father had introduced him to Connie. He went on to say that his father had done yard work for Connie.

I asked Jessie about his dealings with Connie. He said he had purchased some equipment and was doing some landscaping. Connie called him and asked if he would do some work for her, and he agreed. He told me that he worked on the property for a few days and that the work included filling in an old well at Connie's direction. Jessie said his business was beginning to do well, and while he was working on her property, Connie approached him with an offer to do his books and properly set up his business. He said she told him she was a bookkeeper, and he said it sounded like a legitimate offer and accepted.

Connie even offered to let Jessie keep some of his equipment in her barn. Jessie said that things went well for a couple of months, and the business was growing. But then Connie started trying to exercise more control over his business. He said they finally had a showdown about it, with him telling her that this was not working and that it would be best if he looked after his own affairs. Jessie said that Connie went ballistic, and as he left, she attacked his truck with a hammer, damaging it in several places. He said he had to get the sheriff's department to go with him to retrieve his equipment from Connie's property.

I asked Jessie if he could remember the approximate location of the well. He said he could go with me right then to show me where it was. I told him to park his car and to get in with me. We were only mile from the property at 421 Ware's Crossroad. I pulled onto the shoulder of the road at a gate that leads into the pasture next to the house. Jessie pointed out a taller clump of briars on top of the hill approximately one hundred yards from where we were. "Clay," he said, "that well is no more than ten feet from that stand of briars. I filled it in with a Bobcat, and Connie and another lady stood there and watched."

I asked him to describe the well as it had been before he filled it in. Jessie said it was an old hand-dug well three or four feet wide. It had been filled up to about ten feet from the top with different things like tree trash and pieces of wood.

I asked Jessie what he thought about the possibility that Connie had killed Fred. Jessie said that he thought her to be very capable of killing Fred if she felt it was necessary. He didn't mince words: "That woman has the devil in her." I then asked him if he thought she would have needed some help to get his body to the well site. Jessie told me that he had witnessed Connie perform some pretty intense physical labor. He had seen her running a chainsaw, carrying fence posts and handling bags of animal feed like a man.

He also brought up the fact that there was at least one all-terrain vehicle on the property. Jessie estimated the distance from the house to the well was less than one hundred yards. He said, in his opinion, if Connie had killed Fred late Thursday night or early Friday morning, she could have easily gotten the body to the well with the ATV and disposed of it before daylight Friday morning.

I thanked him for his time and told him how grateful I was for what would prove to be valuable information. It would be another key element in unraveling the black widow's web.

15

TIME TO FISH OR CUT BAIT

Considering all I had discovered, I was reasonably sure Connie had killed Fred and that his remains were buried in the old covered well on her property. I felt we had ample probable cause to obtain a search warrant. It was time to make my case to Pete, as he would have the final decision over whether we had enough to proceed at this point.

Pete was out of town on the morning of September 25, 2003. Pete had told me to keep him abreast of my activity, as the case was coming together very rapidly at this point. I had been advising Pete of the progress in the case constantly. I was prepared to make a long and arduous plea in favor of moving forward with the search warrant. I called Pete, and before I could start my protracted argument, he said, "I think you have enough for a search warrant." I was elated.

We went on to discuss how big and complex our undertaking would be upon the issuance of the search warrant. It was going to require a tremendous amount of coordination between several agencies, and someone had to handle the tons of earth that would be moved during the excavation.

I assured Pete that I could handle the necessary logistics of getting that done. He said he was comfortable with that and that he was proud of the progress I had made. He told me to get started on getting a search warrant affidavit and a search warrant together; when I completed them, he wanted me to let one of the assistant DAs review them before I presented them to a judge. He wanted to be sure we had our Is dotted and our Ts crossed, as this would be a one-last-shot operation in finding justice for Fred Wilkerson and exposing the black widow's web.

16

NO ROOM FOR ERROR

We had to be absolutely sure that everything we did from this point had been reviewed, analyzed and checked for any flaws or mistakes. Anything we fell short on could be grounds for appeal, providing we were able to get a conviction at trial.

Judge Allen Keeble had been a superior court judge for many years. I had watched him my entire career. I knew him to be thorough, fair and straightforward. If he had any doubts that our request for the search warrant fell short of what the law required, he would say we didn't have enough. Judge Keeble was not a rubber stamp guy. Knowing that we would be called to account at every turn, Judge Keeble was our man.

I called Debra Taylor, Judge Keeble's secretary, and asked if the judge was in, and she told me he was in his office. I asked if she would check to see if he could spare a few minutes for me. Debra called back and said that the judge invited me over and could see me now if I could come over. In five minutes, I was walking into Judge Keeble's office. Debra announced my arrival, and Judge Keeble invited me back into his office.

I told him I had been looking into the Fred Wilkerson case and had an affidavit for a search warrant that I wanted him to look at and consider. We went on talking as he began reading the affidavit. Then, as he read, he became quiet, and our conversation stopped as he devoted his full attention to the papers in front of him. I could tell as he read that his interest in what he was seeing was piqued.

"Well, it certainly looks like you've done your homework," the judge told me. He complimented me on my efforts in the case and signed the affidavit and search warrant. I exhaled a huge sigh of relief. If my efforts passed muster with Judge Keeble, I was confident we were traveling down a road to resolution.

I knew that the time was soon approaching that my theory of what had happened to Fred Wilkerson would be tested. I had either helped find justice for him or had opened some old wounds once again that would torture his family. I prayed that it was the former and not the latter and that I was on the right track in unraveling the black widow's web.

17

UNDER THE GUN

With Judge Keeble signing the search warrant, we had made it over the first legal hurdle that would allow us to search the Quedenses' property and excavate the old well. A search warrant must be served within ten days of its issue. After that length of time, the information on the affidavit is considered stale, and the affidavit must be updated and resubmitted to the judge for their review to issue another search warrant. To serve an out-of-date search warrant would result in the search being deemed unconstitutional under the Fourth Amendment. This would result in any evidence obtained under the authority of that warrant being deemed inadmissible.

We had a monumental task to coordinate with numerous agencies, experts and government officials, and we had to obtain the equipment and skill necessary to literally move a mountain of earth within ten days.

I had contacted Captain Willis Grizzard at the Troup County Sheriff's Office and advised him that we had a search warrant. I asked him if he would get started on his end with the many issues that we had to address in a very short period. At this point, we had to divide in order to conquer. He was just as excited as I was, and we were ready to get started in our quest to find justice for the Wilkerson family. I was sure we were about to penetrate the black widow's web.

18

IT PAYS TO KNOW SOMEONE
WHO KNOWS WHAT THE HELL THEY'RE
DOING

I have been in a position where I had to poke my nose into other people's business. I have even had to deal with cemetery exhumations to search for evidence, but this was an entirely different animal. We weren't exhuming a coffin whose location and contents we knew. This situation called for, basically, an archaeological search for a body or remains where we were not exactly sure what that search might entail. The knowledge needed to complete this task was far above my paygrade. However, operating under the doctrine that friends are worth more than money, I knew just the man for the job.

On Friday September 26, 2003, I called Dr. Richard "Rick" Snow. Dr. Snow was the forensic anthropologist at the Georgia Bureau of Investigation. Rick had assisted me in a prior case that I had successfully investigated, and we had become friends.

Dr. Snow is a world-renowned forensic anthropologist. He has worked for the United Nations, recovering and identifying bodies from mass graves in Bosnia. He has recovered and identified the remains of U.S. airmen lost in World War II in Germany and those of marines lost in the South Pacific, buried in mass graves on the island of Tarawa. While with the GBI, Dr. Snow was responsible for recovering and identifying 334 bodies from the Tri State Crematory property in Noble, Georgia, in 2005, as well as handling untold numbers of cases involving the recovery and identity of individuals throughout his career. Today, he is the president of

Forensic Anthropology Consulting Services, located in Knoxville, Tennessee, and serves as a consultant to the National Center for Missing and Exploited Children.

Criminal anthropologist Dr. Rick Snow. *Courtesy of Dr. Rick Snow.*

Rick answered my call, exactly as I knew he would: "Clay, what can I help you with?" I briefed him on the case and told him that I strongly suspected the victim's body to be in a covered abandoned well. He said that he had some experience with recovering remains from wells and questioned me about the site's accessibility, the size and suspected depth of the well and the characteristics of the surrounding terrain.

I was able to quickly furnish the information he needed. The well was in an open pasture with excellent access through a gate from a county road. I had been told by neighbors and people familiar with the area that the well was possibly as deep as forty to fifty feet, as it was located on a hilltop.

Dr. Snow asked when this would need to be done; I told him of our urgency due to the fact that the search warrant was already signed and we had only ten days to execute it. To my amazement, Rick said, "How about Tuesday?" He said he would bring his tools and equipment to excavate the cylinder of the well. He said he would need some heavy equipment to dig and clear away the area surrounding the well itself. After that was done, he would excavate the well itself by hand so as not to disturb or damage any evidence that might be located there. Dr. Snow did emphasize just how much dirt was going to need to be moved. For every foot we went down, we'd need to clear a foot away from the well in all directions at the same depth to ensure the safety of Dr. Snow and his team from a possible wall collapse. If the well was excavated to a depth of thirty feet, this would require an excavation that was sixty feet wide and thirty feet deep. I told him I would do whatever it took to have things ready for him upon his arrival. We agreed to meet on the morning of Tuesday, September 30, at 8:00 a.m.

19

CALLING ON AN OLD FRIEND

The magnitude of our undertaking was setting in, and I was becoming nervous about what I had committed myself to do in a very short period. I called Captain Grizzard and brought him up to speed about my conversation with Dr. Snow. He agreed to handle all the security of the scene. Even though we were being very cautious to keep our upcoming operation as quiet as possible, when we showed up with twenty law enforcement vehicles and various pieces of heavy equipment to start an excavation in plain view in a location long rumored to contain a body, we knew this could quickly turn into a spectators' circus.

Grizzard would also attend to the search of the interior of the residence along with a team he would assemble. We would interview Connie together as the excavation took place.

My next task was to procure the equipment and personnel necessary to move the mountain of earth we needed to safely complete our mission. All this activity was taking place on Friday afternoon, giving us only the weekend and one day to get everything into place. It was becoming a bit overwhelming. As my father used to jokingly warn, "Son, don't let your bird dog mouth overload your coon dog ass." I felt as if, any minute, I'd start howling. I knew I was going to need some help from my and Fred's old friend.

Raymon Vaughan had, through a lifetime of hard work and support from his family, acquired considerable wealth. His trucking business had been very successful, and as his business expanded, he collected a fairly extensive array of the sort of heavy equipment we would need to get this job done.

I called Raymon and asked to meet with him, and he readily agreed. I met him at one of his warehouses. As I told him of the progress I had made on the case of his missing friend, he responded in disbelief. Raymon asked if I really thought his friend was there. I told him the good news: I was absolutely confident that we were going to locate Fred. I then told Raymon the bad news: things had moved so fast that I hadn't yet gotten anyone to help with the excavation.

As I knew he would, Raymon immediately volunteered to fill the bill. He asked what we would need. I told him we needed a large excavator, a large dozer or loader and a lowboy to get them to the site. Raymon said, "Boy, if that's the only problem you got then you ain't got no problem." We went on to talk about the things Dr. Snow said would need to be done. When I asked what this was going to cost, Raymon seemed a bit agitated and said he wasn't doing this for money, it was for an old friend. Truthfully, I exhaled a sigh of relief when Raymon said he expected no payment. What he had agreed to do for nothing would have cost a few thousand dollars to the district attorney's office and the people of Troup County. And if it turned out to be fruitless, I was going to be anointed with a large amount of egg on my face.

We agreed to meet just before 8:00 a.m. on Tuesday morning, just down the road from the site. He said he'd be there with everything we needed. Yes, indeed, friends are worth more than money.

20

LOOSE ENDS

The one thing I had not yet done was alert Tim and Tracie of our intentions. I had been keeping them informed on my progress, but I hadn't yet advised them of our Tuesday plan, simply because I feared we might not be able to get everything in place. The last thing I wanted to do was fail to fulfill a commitment to them. Those two souls had experienced enough disappointment in the last seventeen years, and I wasn't about to add to it.

But at last, I thought we had our ducks in a row. I went by West Georgia Paint and Body late that Friday afternoon and informed Tim of our plan to execute the search warrant on Tuesday. I asked him to tell Tracie and her husband, Roger Campbell, of the events that were about to take place. I also asked that he not tell anyone outside the family of our intentions, as we wanted to maintain the element of surprise.

Monday found me checking with everyone involved to be sure that nothing had changed that would interrupt our plan—that everyone was clear on their responsibilities to ensure that everything would go smoothly and according to plan.

I met with Pete and assured him that everything was on track. He congratulated me on what we had accomplished. He went on to say that the sheriff had expressed some concerns about the way the next day's events would play out and that he thought it would be best if I stayed up at the residence and not come down to the excavation site. I understood the political dynamics, and it was fine with me. Pete planned to stay at the office early and come to the site as the search was progressing.

Monday night found me tossing and turning all night. I don't think I slept for more than thirty minutes. All I could think about were the what-ifs: What if Fred wasn't there? What if we found nothing in the search? What if we didn't answer the questions we sought to answer? What if I had done nothing but open old wounds that would extend the suffering of Fred's family?

I was looking at the clock with nervous anticipation when the alarm went off Tuesday morning. I knew that in the next few hours, we would have answers to all the what-ifs that had tortured me all night. We would either have suffered a gut-wrenching defeat or successfully destructed the black widow's web.

21

A DAY OF RECKONING

September 30, 2003, would prove to be a day of reckoning indeed—the only question was: for whom? There were two distinct possibilities: either our search would be successful, and Connie Quedens would be held accountable for her heinous crime, or if not, I would have orchestrated an exercise in total futility, wasting thousands of dollars in resources and manpower for which I would fall under intense scrutiny and cause the district attorney's office to come under a great deal of public criticism. No matter what the outcome, the time had come for those questions to be answered.

The day started just as we had planned; everyone was present and on time. We discussed details of everyone's responsibilities. Assisting Dr. Snow from the GBI were Agent and Crime Scene Specialist Tony Lima and Agents Vaughn Estes and Terry Hunt. Dr. Snow would direct operations at the excavation. Raymon had brought his son Terry Vaughan and Ellis Hyatt, both seasoned equipment operators. Together, they would work under the direction of Dr. Snow in order to safely excavate the contents of the well. A contingent of deputies would maintain security around the scene. Captain Grizzard and I would serve the search warrant at the residence and interview Connie. We would maintain radio contact with Dr. Snow's team as the excavation progressed.

Dr. Snow's team, along with Raymon and all his heavy equipment and several marked patrol cars, stopped on the road by the gate. Captain Grizzard and I proceeded to the residence and knocked on the door. The door was

A view of the well site from Ware's Cross Road. *Author's collection.*

A view showing the distance from the laundry room door to the well site. *Author's collection.*

Excavation equipment arriving at the search scene. *Author's collection.*

Work progressing at the excavation site. *Author's collection.*

Raymon Vaughan and Ellis Hyatt discussing progress at the excavation site. *Courtesy of Sonia Vaughan.*

answered by a man who identified himself as Terry Burris—unknown to us, he was living in the house with Connie. When we asked to speak to Connie, Burris informed us that she was at "the Salvation Army," doing her Christian work. We asked him if he could call her and tell her we were there, as she was needed at home. We radioed Dr. Snow's team and told them to stand by and not enter the property until Quedens arrived.

Connie arrived shortly thereafter. We introduced ourselves, and I told Connie we were there to execute a search warrant of the property in regard to the disappearance of Fred Wilkerson. I read her the warrant and provided her with a copy. Connie said that she had nothing to hide and that she had been questioned before without anything turning up. "You didn't need a warrant; you can search all you like," she said. Knowing that should she contest the validity of the search warrant, her voluntary consent would

Dr. Rick Snow and Agent Vaughn Estes recovering remains from the well. *Author's collection.*

Dr. Rick Snow, Agents Terry Hunt and Vaughn Estes and Troup County coroner Jeff Cook recovering remains from the excavation site. *Author's collection.*

Laurie Wilkerson, Tim Wilkerson, Ramon Vaughan, Tracie Campbell and Roger Campbell looking on as the excavation of the well continues. *Author's collection.*

Uncovering remains at the excavation site. *Author's collection.*

Skeletal remains hauled up from the well. *Author's collection.*

Skeletal remains hauled up from the well. *Author's collection.*

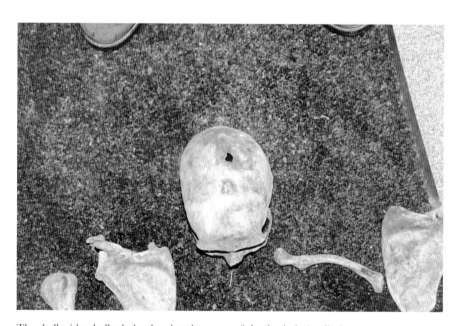

The skull with a bullet hole, showing the cause of death. *Author's collection.*

supersede the search warrant, I asked her to sign a consent to search, which, to my astonishment, she did.

I informed her that we would be executing the warrant and that the search would begin with the excavation of the old well in the pasture. Connie replied with an ice-cold stare, "If he's down there, I don't know anything about it." With that, I gave the excavation team the go-ahead to enter the property and start their work. The excavation began at approximately 9:30 a.m. Captain Grizzard and I sat with Connie; at this point, she was not in custody and was free to leave if she saw fit. But she stayed, and after a while, her demeanor began to change; she went from having an air of confident arrogance to being in a state of marked anxiety.

22

AN EVER-EVOLVING SAGA

We sat with Connie in her living room, and it was obvious that she was becoming increasingly anxious. She would get out of her chair and pace nervously around the room before sitting back down and then repeating the process. I thought now would be the time to start posing some questions and confront her with some major inconsistencies that I had discovered in her stories concerning her contact with Fred Wilkerson around the time of his disappearance. I asked why she had not gone to Florida with Gary and the boys that Thanksgiving weekend. She stated that at the last minute, she had been required to work on Friday and Saturday at the Honda dealership, where she was employed. I asked her if she had gone anywhere other than to work over that weekend. She said she had only gone to a work gathering at Knickers in LaGrange on Friday evening. I reiterated: "To work and that trip to Knickers are the only times you left your house while Gary and the boys were gone?" She stated flatly, "Yes, the only times."

I told Connie that I had read the statement she had given in December 1987, the first time she was questioned about Fred's disappearance. She had said then that prior to Fred's disappearance, the last time she had seen or spoken to him was at the funeral of a mutual friend, George Boykin, approximately a month prior.

I pointed out to Connie that in her sworn testimony in the probate action she had brought to have Fred declared dead, she had testified that after she had been served with the lawsuit filed by Fred just prior to his disappearance, she called him to discuss a possible resolution. At this point, Connie displayed a degree of frustration and said she had simply forgotten about the phone call.

I felt like it was time to confront her with my ace in the hole. I told Connie that I had a witness who had stated "you had requested her to pick you up at the Atlanta airport on the Saturday after Thanksgiving 1987, the weekend that Fred disappeared." I told her I found it odd that if, in fact, the witness was correct, she had picked Connie up no more than one hundred yards from where Fred's car had been located.

You could see the terror in Connie's eyes, and after a moment of silence, she stammered and began to relate what I can only describe as a rambling fairy tale.

She said on the night of Thanksgiving 1987, she had called Fred and asked him to come over so they could discuss a possible resolution to the lawsuit. She stated that when Fred arrived, she was in the laundry room, cutting pipe to use as closet rods. She said when Fred drove up, he pulled into the garage and, as he did, a marked police car pulled in behind him. She said she could not make out the agency. A uniformed officer got out, along with a woman in a nurse's uniform. Connie said a loud argument erupted between them and Fred. At some point, Fred got into the car with them, and they drove off. She said she never saw Fred again. The next day, she got a call from the person she supposed Fred had left with. She was told that if she didn't take Fred's car to the airport and leave it there, she'd never see her children alive again. She said that she called Lisa Hulderman and had her pick her up at the airport where she had left Fred's car. Connie went on to say that she had taken the car to the airport as instructed, but she didn't kill Fred.

When I asked Connie why she never reported any of this to law enforcement, I found her answer ridiculous to the point of being comical. With that deer in the headlights look, Connie said the man in uniform that night looked like Captain Willis Grizzard, and she had been afraid to report what she had seen. Captain Grizzard's expression was one of utter amazement in reaction to her comment. Connie had just replaced seventeen years of lies with an outrageous fairy tale.

My dad always said the problem with a lie is that you will always have to tell another one to cover the previous lie, and you will, at some point, have told so many lies that you can't keep up with them and they will start to contradict each other. Connie now found herself in that situation. Now, everything she said about Fred's disappearance was totally contradictory to everything she had said before.

I could only sit in disbelief after hearing Connie's bizarre account of the events surrounding Fred's disappearance. It would be her own outrageous ramblings that would signal the impending unraveling of the black widow's web.

23

A GRIM DISCOVERY

I sat in a daze, trying to process the dramatic turn of events. Connie's nonsensical account of the night Fred disappeared was mind numbing. She had no sooner gotten through with her outrageous tale than the portable radio crackled to life.

Word came from the team at the excavation: "We have human remains." It was just after 10:30 a.m. The team had been working for only a little over an hour. The skeletal remains were located in an inverted position seventeen feet down in the well.

There had been trash and debris dumped in the well, some of which was charred, consistent with Lisa Hulderman's statement of the attempted fire. The remains were found rolled in a piece of charred carpet, consistent with that from the laundry room in the basement, where Connie said she had been cutting off closet rods.

Encased in the carpet were the skeletal remains, still in the clothes Fred had been wearing. Located in the jeans pocket were a ring of keys and a tube of ChapStick. Also in the carpet was a rusted hacksaw and several pieces of cut pipe.

Dr. Snow's work was just beginning. He now had to recover all of the skeletal remains, catalog them and rebuild the skeleton in its proper anatomical position to ensure complete recovery before the remains were bagged and recorded as evidence. Dr. Snow noted that there were several fractures to bones that would be consistent with dumping debris on top of the body. The single most telling injury was one to the skull. Located in the back of the skull was an elongated hole. Dr. Snow described this as a keyhole defect indicative of an execution-style gunshot from behind the victim. He stated that he had seen many of these injuries in the remains of the victims of mass executions in Bosnia. He went on to say these findings were preliminary, but he felt sure that this was the injury that ended this victim's life.

When asked if the contents of the pockets were consistent with items that his father would have had, Tim indicated the keys appeared to be Fred's work keys and that his father always carried a tube of ChapStick in his pocket. Ironically, as Fred was building the house, Tim, while helping his father, had often carried construction debris to the well and thrown it in.

It was a bittersweet discovery for Tim and Tracie; as tragic as the truth was, it ended what seemed like a lifetime of suspicion and uncertainty. They would soon be able to lay Fred to rest in the dignified manner he deserved. Finally, it appeared as if someone was going to be held accountable for the senseless killing of their father.

But there was still much work to be done by us to ensure that the black widow now fell victim to her own web of greed, lies, deceit and murder.

24

ABOUT TIME

Pete said that if we found the body, we would, at that point, place Connie under arrest on probable cause and sign warrants later.

The spectator circus that we were concerned about had developed just as we suspected. There were at least two hundred people lining Ware's Crossroad in front of the property, along with three television news satellite trucks. Fred's family, friends, neighbors and some plain curiosity seekers all stood, waiting for what they were about to see.

Above and opposite: Connie Quedens being led to a patrol car after her arrest for the murder of Fred Wilkerson. *Author's collection.*

As soon as the news about the discovery of the remains from Dr. Snow's team sank in, a feeling of satisfaction and accomplishment swept over me. We were standing in the living room—myself, Captain Grizzard, Deputy Terri Wood and Connie. I turned to Connie and said, "Connie Quedens, you are under arrest for the murder of Fred Wilkerson." I advised her of her Miranda rights and placed her in handcuffs; the deputy led her outside and placed her in a waiting patrol car.

As the patrol car pulled away from the house, people lined both sides of the road. They began cheering and applauding. It was indeed a spectacle like I had never seen before, and I was damned glad to be a part of it. All the time and effort we had put in the case had been worth it. It was about long-awaited justice, and it was about time it was served. I hoped Fred was listening and knew he and his family had finally been freed from the black widow's web.

25

UNBELIEVABLE FINDS

There was still much work to be done, even after the morning's grim discovery. We knew at this point that the house was now a crime scene, and the search of the home was now of the utmost importance. The fact that the crime was committed some seventeen years prior didn't diminish the fact that the house could hold valuable evidence of the crime.

Captain Grizzard, along with GBI crime specialist agent Tony Lima, conducted a thorough search of the house. Their findings would prove invaluable to the prosecution of the case.

I'm not sure what led Connie to do the things she did. I saw her as somewhat of an enigma. In some things, she was cunning and meticulous; in others, I at first thought she was careless. The more I got to know her, however, my opinion changed. Connie was arrogant, narcissistic and evil. The things I at first considered careless or sloppy weren't that at all. Connie reveled in the evil things she had done and had no remorse whatsoever for any of her actions.

As sick as it sounds, I think she liked having trophies to remind her of her deeds. Some of these trophies would contribute to her undoing. In the laundry room where she killed Fred, there were still signs of blood spatter on the wall consistent with castoff from a gunshot wound. She had kept the invoice she got when she ordered replacement carpet for the laundry room. The search of the home also revealed several firearms in the house, which were illegal for Connie to possess, as she was a convicted felon.

There was one find in particular that, when I heard of it, absolutely flabbergasted me. Captain Grizzard called me the day after the search was complete. He said, "You're not going to believe this; we found two audio cassette tapes you have got to hear." Connie and Gary were again going through a divorce, and the tape was of Connie making settlement demands regarding the divorce. Connie said, "I want my Walther pistol." Gary replied, "Connie, there were only three Walther pistols. The two with consecutive serial numbers I bought from Marcus Smith for the boys and the one that someone may have used at Fred's time that you had me get rid of."

As damning as the first tape was, it paled in comparison to the second one. It was a tape Connie had recorded after she was served with Fred's lawsuit just before he disappeared. It was a profanity-laced tirade demanding an explanation of why he filed it. Fred replied weakly, "I had to." At that point, Connie screamed prophetically, "Fred Wilkerson, you son of a bitch, I will kill you!"

For Connie to keep such damning evidence was indicative of the fact that she believed she could never be caught. In her unbridled arrogance, she relished the idea that she was sure she had gotten away with murder.

Connie Quedens was soon to find out that the sinister web she had spun was about to entangle and consume her.

26

SOMETIMES YOU DEAL WITH THE DEVIL TO GET THE WITCH

The search of the house had produced several damning key pieces of evidence. The one that absolutely had to be pursued was the recording between Gary and Connie regarding the pistol. We had to talk to Gary Quedens.

I contacted Gary and told him we needed to meet with him in reference to our investigation. On October 26, 2003, we met at the Troup County Sheriff's Office. Present for the interview were me, Special Agent Terry Hunt, Captain Willis Grizzard, Sheriff Donny Turner, Gary Quedens and his attorney Robert Whatley.

Gary Quedens stated that when he returned from Florida with the boys, he found a pistol on the floor of the basement. He said he asked Connie what it was doing there. Gary stated that Connie said he needed to get rid of it, as something had happened here and "we don't need to be implicated." Gary further stated that when he became aware of Fred's disappearance, he suspected Connie had killed him.

When asked about the well, Gary said that Connie began saying the well needed to be filled in before one of the kids fell in and that she would attend to it. When asked what had happened to the pistol, Gary Quedens stated he had kept the pistol until the next gun show in Columbus, at which time he sold it.

From the statement he gave and the contents of the taped recording, we were sure that Gary reasonably believed Connie had been involved in the killing of Fred Wilkerson.

At this point, one has to assume one of two things: either Gary was just like Fred and had been and was under the spell of a manipulative, evil woman or he was aware of everything Connie was doing and acquiesced to her actions by willingly contributing to the coverup in order to participate in the financial gains sought by Connie. Gary had to either be just as gullible as Fred or just as evil as Connie.

I don't think Gary was afraid of Connie. If he was sleeping in a house with a woman he suspected had killed her lover, common sense would tell him he was in just as much jeopardy as Fred had been. But on the other hand, common sense should have told him that finding the gun on the floor was an attempt by Connie to frame him for the crime. How could he reconcile those things? To me, the jury is still out on these facts. One thing is certain: he did willingly dispose of a gun that, by his own admission, he thought was used to kill Fred Wilkerson. Gary benefited from the fact that our commitment to convict Connie for her horrendous crime outweighed our desire to punish him for his lesser crime. The truth was that we needed his testimony to bolster our case against Connie. Without it, Connie's defense attorney would surely have raised the question about whether Gary had been a viable suspect in the crime.

I was able to substantiate the fact that from Wednesday to Sunday on Thanksgiving weekend 1987, Gary and his boys were in Port Richey, Florida. Just days prior to the trip, Gary had purchased a new car from Larry Rich Nissan in LaGrange. While in Florida, the car experienced a serious mechanical failure on Thanksgiving Day. A local dealership in Tampa arranged a dealer swap with Larry Rich, and on Saturday, Gary picked up the new vehicle in Florida. This proved his whereabouts at the time of Fred's murder.

At this point, we were presented with a dilemma. Would we charge Gary for his involvement in covering up the crime of murder and as a party to the crime of murder, or would his testimony be more valuable to the prosecution of the person who we knew had actually committed the murder? After a great deal of soul searching and evaluating what we had—and with Pete's advice—we elected to go with the latter. Gary Quedens was arrested and charged with tampering with evidence. He was offered immunity regarding the murder of Fred Wilkerson in return for his truthful testimony against Connie at trial.

I felt conflicted by the fact that, by his own admission, Gary Quedens had withheld information that I felt he had a moral obligation to divulge, information that could have resulted in the resolution of this case long ago and the relief of years of suffering for Fred's family. The probative value of his testimony, however, was great to the prosecution of the person directly responsible for the murder of Fred Wilkerson.

Sometimes, as unfair as it seems, life requires that you pick the lesser of two evils; sometimes, you deal with the devil to get the witch.

27

ANTICIPATING THE DEFENSE

In order to have a successful prosecution, one must anticipate the defense and be prepared to combat it beforehand.

We knew that one of the primary defenses that would be raised at trial was uncertainty of the identification of the remains. In 2003, the science of DNA testing was still evolving, as it is today. In order to establish as near a conclusive identity of the remains recovered from the well as possible, Dr. Snow extracted samples of mitochondrial DNA from the large bones and teeth of the skeleton. Mitochondrial DNA is a DNA sequence that follows the maternal lineage of a person. We had no known DNA from Fred Wilkerson. We were able to obtain a DNA sample from a known relative of Fred Wilkerson, Jane Hendrix, a daughter of his sister, Jewell.

What the lab results revealed was that Jane Hendrix and the remains recovered from the well on the Quedenses' property came from a common maternal line. This, along with the physical evidence recovered with the skeletal remains, ensured a positive identity of the remains being those of Fred Wilkerson. There was ample precedent for the admission of the DNA results, and it would most likely be admitted into evidence.

The admission of the audio tapes recovered from Connie's home would surely be objected to by the defense. But we knew that they were the product of a legal search, and they, too, were likely to be admitted into evidence. If admitted, they would be damning evidence of premeditation. Nothing could be more impactful to a jury than hearing the defendant, in her own words, state her intentions.

As for the canceled checks written by Connie on Fred's life for the entire seven-year period leading up to the time Fred was declared dead, they would also point to motive.

The prosecution also sought to enter into evidence the entire skeletal remains of Fred Wilkerson. They would be placed in the anatomically correct position on a gurney and wheeled into the courtroom by our expert witness as a visual aid. The defense would object to this on the grounds that the presence of the skeletal remains alone was prejudicial and inflammatory, thus outweighing its evidentiary value. Our position would be that it was necessary to assist Dr. Snow in his presentation to the jury about the remains' identification and cause of death.

These and other questions of law concerning evidence admissibility were answered in pretrial motions by Judge William Lee. Judge Lee served as senior judge of the five-county Coweta Judicial Circuit. Judge Lee was a no-nonsense, experienced jurist; his rulings were rarely contested on appeal, and when they were, the appeals were almost never successful. The case was in the hands of a fair and competent judge.

The Jackson-Denno evidentiary hearing held pretrial by Judge Lee resulted in the admission of all evidence requested by the state. The stage was set for the legal showdown that would determine Connie Quedens's fate. Questions of fact would ultimately be answered by twelve enlightened jurors. There were several factual questions the defense would surely put into play before the jury. They would contend that Connie had no motive to kill Fred Wilkerson. The prosecution, however, would contend that she had roughly thirty-seven thousand reasons to kill Fred. The defense would contend that Connie was physically incapable of completing the elements of this crime. These and other issues of fact would be put before the jury for them to decide if Connie Quedens had, beyond a reasonable doubt, murdered Fred Wilkerson and disposed of his body by placing it in that well.

Pete was a master of judging his cases. The old adage that sometimes less is more applies to cases at trial. Pete was a firm believer in the "KISS" method. Comically, the acronym stands for "keep it simple, stupid." Many times in my career, I have seen prosecutors and defense attorneys alike have a simple factual case that they would have won if only they had presented the evidence in a way the jury could follow and understand. Their mistake was getting overly technical and complicated, losing the jury's ability to follow the evidence. It only takes one confused juror to hang the jury, resulting in a mistrial.

Pete would never fall victim to that age-old trap. He was not one of those lawyers who just liked to talk to hear his own voice. He knew he had sufficient evidence. He would factually present the evidence and let the jury do its job.

It was an intricate chess game that would play out at trial. I felt sure that I had provided Pete with everything he needed to achieve check and checkmate.

28

A PROMISE TO KEEP

onnie Quedens spent the next thirteen months in the Troup County Jail, awaiting trial. The trial was set for November 1, 2004, before Judge William Lee. We had worked diligently to ensure our case was as airtight as possible. One never knows with absolute certainty what a jury might do. I was confident that we would find justice for Fred Wilkerson and his family.

A few weeks before we were scheduled to go to trial, I received a call from Tim and Tracie's mother, Carolyn; she asked if I could drop by her house and speak with her. Of course, I agreed to come right over. Since Fred's disappearance, Carolyn had helped Tim develop his business and was a great part of his success. She was very much involved in the lives of Tracie, her husband, Roger, and her grandchildren. She had been remarried to Fred Alsabrook, and they shared a good life together.

Sadly, Carolyn had been diagnosed with cancer, and her health was failing. When I arrived at the house, Fred met me at the door, and we went into the den, where Carolyn was lying on the sofa. She needlessly apologized for not getting up to meet me. We spoke a few minutes, and she then said she had witnessed her children agonize over the loss of their father all these years. The pain she had seen them endure had tortured her. She thanked me for the work I had done on the case. Through tears, she said that she was afraid she would never live to see justice for her children; she asked if I really thought we'd convict Connie for Fred's murder and all the suffering she had caused her children.

I was fighting back tears myself, trying to keep my composure. In a breaking voice, I said, "Mrs. Carolyn, I promise you with what we have, it will take the jury longer to elect a foreman than it will to convict her." She looked at me, weakly smiled and again thanked me for what I had done. We said goodbye, and I left thinking to myself, "God, please don't let me have lied." Carolyn was right: she would not live to see the trial. A few days after my visit, she passed away, surrounded by her loved ones. I knew that was a conversation I'd never forget and a promise I somehow had to keep.

29

THE TRIAL

It was with much anticipation that I awaited the trial of Connie Quedens. I felt we had done everything possible to secure a positive outcome. Over the years, I had been involved in and witnessed many jury trials. The one thing that is certain is that you can never be 100 percent sure what a jury might do.

We had an excellent and experienced prosecutor in Pete Skandalakis. He was well prepared and confident in our case. On the other side of the aisle, Connie had hired an excellent defense attorney, Arthur "Skin" Edge. Connie had made an excellent choice. Edge was then practicing out of Newnan, Georgia, had served as a state senator, was a hometown product of LaGrange and had an excellent reputation for winning for his clients.

The trial began in front of Judge Lee on November 1, 2004. The first day was taken up with jury selection. The process went smoothly, and by late afternoon, we had seated twelve primary jurors and two alternates.

Day two began with opening statements. Pete, in a powerful opening, laid out the prosecution's case in a preview of what the state would set out to prove. Skin Edge attacked the state's case as being totally circumstantial, with Connie being the victim of an overzealous prosecution. He also argued that Connie was totally physically incapable of committing the crime.

As the trial progressed, Pete presented myriad pieces of evidence against Connie, including copies of checks on Fred's life insurance policy, which were written by Connie from the time of Fred's disappearance until she filed

A copy of a check written by Connie Quedens to State Farm Insurance for the semiannual payment for Fred Wilkerson's life insurance policy after she killed him. *Author's collection.*

to have him declared dead to collect the premium seven years later—just like putting money in the bank.

The testimonial evidence included testimony from myself, as I gave a general overview of the case and the information I had gathered during the investigation, including my interview of Connie on the day of the search.

Captain Grizzard also testified to the interview with Connie and the information that laid the foundation for the admission of evidence acquired from the search.

Retired GBI agent Roy Olinger testified to early events in the case and to the fact that Fred's car had been located at the Atlanta airport.

Gary Quedens testified to returning from Florida, finding a gun on the floor of the basement and having Connie tell him to dispose of it.

Tim Wilkerson and Tracie Wilkerson Campbell gave emotional details of their dad's disappearance and details that strengthened the positive identification of their father's remains. They also testified to their knowledge of the romantic and financial relationship between their father and Connie Quedens.

Joan Hulderman testified to the conversation she had with Connie, in which she stated she wouldn't be making the trip to Florida with the rest of the family because she had to stay to protect her property.

Guerin Quedens testified to his mother's volatile personality. He also recalled conversations between Gary and Connie about the disposal of the gun. He also recounted that, at the last minute, Connie had decided not to accompany them to Florida and that, upon their return, his father had found the gun on the basement floor.

Jessie Patterson testified that Connie Quedens had employed him to fill in the well. He also stated that he had witnessed Connie Quedens involved in activity that he described as heavy manual labor. He also testified that there was an all-terrain vehicle that he saw on the property while doing work; he said it could have been used to drag the carpet containing the body of Fred Wilkerson the relatively short distance to the well.

The jury was brought to the edge of their seats as they listened intently to Lisa Hulderman Miles recount the events of the Saturday she picked Connie up at the airport, where Fred's car had been found. She also testified that Connie, shortly after the trip to the airport, had gotten her and several of her friends to drag brush to the old well, where Connie had attempted to set fire to its contents.

Dr. Snow was qualified by the court as an expert witness. He described the process of discovery and recovery of the remains. He explained all the methods they used to ensure the true identity of the remains. Dr. Snow also testified that the skull had a gunshot wound that had resulted in the death of the victim. He described the injury as a keyhole defect, similar to the wounds found on the remains of victims of mass executions he excavated in Bosnia. He said the wound was the result of a single gunshot from a steep angle directly behind the victim to the back of the head. Dr. Snow also described the process used to extract a DNA sample from the remains.

Megan Clement, an expert in the field of DNA analysis for Lab Corp Incorporated, testified that she had received a mitochondrial DNA sample from the remains recovered by Dr. Snow and a known DNA sample from Jane Hendrix. She explained the process of comparing the two samples. Clement then stated that, in her expert opinion, both samples had DNA consistent with the same maternal lineage. Jane Hendrix was the child of Fred's sister, Jewell. Clement stated that, in her opinion, the remains in the well came from the same maternal source as Jane and Jewell, and those results, coupled with other pieces of evidence found along with the remains, resulted in a positive identification of the remains as being those of Willie Fred Wilkerson.

With a firm foundation laid for its admission, Pete submitted into evidence the tape of Connie and Fred that was recorded immediately after Connie had been served with the lawsuit. The courtroom was deathly quiet as the recording played. Connie, in a profanity-laced tirade, screamed hysterically at Fred, demanding he tell her just what the hell he thought he was doing. Fred answered sheepishly, "I had to." The faces of the jury could not hide the shock of what followed, as Connie again screamed, "Fred Wilkerson, you son of a bitch, I'll kill you!"

Edge did all he could to confront the mountain of evidence on cross-examination. When the defense presented its case, it was primarily based on the fact that Connie didn't have the physical ability to commit the crime and dispose of the body as the state contended. Connie did not take the stand.

Pete's closing argument was emotional and masterful as he laid out the motive and what the state had proven. He said that Connie Quedens had spun a web of lies and deceit that had entrapped Fred Wilkerson into a relationship that resulted in his financial ruin and destroyed his family. He said that when, in her mind, Fred had the audacity to try to recover a small portion of what he had lost, she enticed him, one last time, to come to her house to discuss the lawsuit situation. Once Fred was there, Connie lured him downstairs with a tale of her difficulty in cutting those closet rods, and one last time, in true Fred fashion, Fred got on his knees and began to saw on the pipe, just as he always had responded to Connie's schemes. As he went about doing her bidding, Connie stepped behind him, raised her Walther pistol and cold-heartedly fired a lone bullet into the back of his head, killing him instantly. Then she, having all night and the means necessary, was able to drag the body the approximately seventy-five yards to the well, where she callously dumped it in.

Connie Quedens at the defense table as the jury returns from deliberations. *Courtesy of Shane Frailey.*

Connie then enlisted an unknowing Lisa Hulderman to assist in getting rid of the car. She put the gun on the floor of the basement, where Gary found it and picked it up, placing his fingerprints on the murder weapon, just in case her plan was discovered. He was the perfect suspect as the jealous husband seeking revenge.

In an absolute display of her materialistic greed, Connie continued to pay the premiums on Fred's life insurance policy for the next seven years, knowing every day Fred was lying in the bottom of the well, where she had put him. She did this with the intent to collect the proceeds of the policy of the man she had ruthlessly murdered.

The defense's closing argument basically called into question whether the state had met the burden of proof to convict Connie Quedens for the murder of Fred Wilkerson beyond a reasonable doubt. The jury would have the final say about whether the case had been made.

Judge Lee gave charging instructions to the jury on the fourth day of the trial. It took the jury less than two hours to render a verdict. They found Connie Quedens guilty of malice murder and possession of a firearm by a convicted felon.

The Wilkerson family erupted in emotion at the verdict. The courtroom was brought to order. Judge Lee elected to pass her sentence immediately. He sentenced Connie to life in prison for the murder of Fred Wilkerson.

The scene in the courtroom was one of jubilation, as the Wilkerson family, through tears of joy and relief, thanked the members of the jury for their just verdict. I breathed a sigh of relief knowing that we had accomplished what we set out to do. Fred's remains would be returned to his family, and he would receive the Christian burial he had long been denied. I couldn't help but think of Carolyn, and I hoped she somehow knew my promise to her had been kept. I hoped that she and my dad were smiling down on us for what we had done.

IN RETROSPECT

I n life, all fall short at one time or another, and we all make mistakes; some have greater consequences than others. No one sets out to intentionally take the wrong path in search of the truth, but sometimes, we do. I have.

History is the judge of us all, and to quote the cliché, "It is what it is." We can't change it. I hope that when I fall short, there will be someone who can right the ship and send it sailing in the right direction. This case taught me a lesson: sometimes people are so afraid of being perceived as wrong or falling short that they let it affect the future.

I felt there were some people whom I considered friends or colleagues who would have been more satisfied if I had never gotten involved in the case. I never set out to disprove anything or to place blame; I only wanted to find justice for some people who deserved it, and I was damn proud to have played a part in in finding justice for Fred Wilkerson and his family.

I was criticized by some for shedding light on why the case had stalled in the beginning and gone cold. The facts of the case spoke for themselves. The sheriff at the time, whom I considered a friend, never spoke to me again. If we had not revisited those failures, Fred would still be in that well, and Connie would still be spinning webs and ruining lives. I make no apologies for my actions. Pride is a necessary ingredient to success; however, pride and vanity to excess can be poisonous ingredients in the recipe of life, especially when they negatively affect the lives of others.

In my career, I have had the displeasure of dealing with some very bad people. I had never dealt with anyone as conniving or ruthless as Connie Quedens. Her crimes were not those of passion or opportunity. She contrived long-term objectives that she sought without compassion or sympathy for her victims. Connie was capable of anything up to and including murder to satisfy her insatiable greed.

I can't—and never will be able to—understand how a person can not only take the life of an innocent person but be callous enough to lay their head on a pillow at night less than one hundred yards from where their victim lies. I guess it takes the same kind of person who is conniving enough to enact a long-term scheme to enrich herself from her despicable actions—the same person who is willing to inflict unspeakable, never-ending pain on an innocent family, who is willing to go to any length to satisfy her narcissistic, insatiable greed. That same person has to be possessed by an unspeakable evil. That person is Connie Quedens.

Connie, to this day, has never accepted any responsibility for her crimes or expressed any remorse for her actions. She is currently incarcerated in the Pulaski State Prison in Hawkinsville, Georgia. If justice is truly served, she will spend her last days there. On March 27, 2006, Connie Quedens's appeal was denied in a unanimous decision by the Georgia Supreme Court, and her sentence was upheld. Due to the callous nature of her crimes, she has consistently been denied parole.

It is my sincere hope that when she leaves prison, she has only one more stop to make—and the devil needs to know he's got some serious competition coming. If he's not careful, he just might find himself entangled and consumed in the black widow's web.

During the course of this investigation, I ran across some interesting information. According to law enforcement sources who were contacted in West Virginia regarding this investigation, during the time Connie attended a community college in West Virginia, a professor who was rumored to have been having an affair with a student disappeared, never to be heard from again. The only evidence found in the case was his vehicle, which was located at the Richmond airport.

After Fred disappeared, Connie's oldest son, Garrett, left home and moved to Nashville, where he met, fell in love with and married a Malaysian woman. It was reported that Connie was upset by that turn of events. After a weekend visit home to LaGrange, Garrett became extremely ill and was admitted to the Vanderbilt Medical Center in Nashville, where, only in his mid-twenties, he passed away from cardiac arrest and organ failure. It was reported that Connie collected on a life insurance policy as a result of his death. After speaking with the medical examiner, I learned that no further testing had been done on Garrett's remains at the time of his death, as there had been no reason to suspect foul play. After our conversation, I was told the symptoms he presented could have been consistent with ethylene-glycol poisoning.

It may be a case of unfortunate coincidence—or maybe not. Only one person knows if there are other victims of the black widow's web.

ABOUT THE AUTHOR

Lewis Clayton "Clay" Bryant was born and raised in Troup County, Georgia, and began his career in law enforcement in 1973 as a radio operator with the Georgia State Patrol. In 1976, at the age of twenty-one, he became the youngest trooper with the Georgia State Patrol. In 1980, he became the police chief of Hogansville and remained in that position for twelve years until he resigned in 1992 and went into the private sector. He has been recognized as the most prolific cold case investigator in the United States for single-event homicides. His cases have been chronicled on *48 Hours Investigates*, Bill Kurtis's *Cold Case Files* and Discovery ID's *Murder Book* and has been featured in the *Atlanta Journal Constitution* and in articles in many local and regional newspapers. Bryant resides in LaGrange. This is his second book.